FAITH–SHAPED KIDS

FAITH-SHAPED KIDS

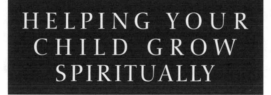

HELPING YOUR
CHILD GROW
SPIRITUALLY

STEVE & VALERIE BELL

MOODY PRESS
CHICAGO

All Scripture quotations, unless otherwise indicated, are taken from the *Holy Bible, New International Version*®. NIV®. Copyright © 1973, 1978, 1984 by International Bible Society. Used by permission of Zondervan Publishing House. All rights reserved.

Scripture quotations marked CEV are taken from the *Contemporary English Version*. Copyright © 1995 by the American Bible Society. Used by permission.

Scripture quotations marked TLB are taken from *The Living Bible* copyright © 1971. Used by permission of Tyndale House Publishers, Inc., Wheaton, Illinois 60189. All rights reserved.

Scripture quotations marked KJV are taken from the King James Version.

Scripture quotations marked AMP are taken from *The Amplified Bible*. Copyright © 1965, 1987 by The Zondervan Corporation. The Amplified New Testament copyright © 1958, 1987 by The Lockman Foundation. Used by permission.

ISBN: 0-8024-3098-8

1 3 5 7 9 10 8 6 4 2

Printed in the United States of America

To our children—
Brendan and his wife, Kailey,
And Justin—
and to our unborn grandchildren . . .
the generations of little ones yet to come.
We pray that each one will be
A living link in our family chain of faith.

118|

CONTENTS

ACKNOWLEDGMENTS

Every book project takes on a life of its own. *Faith-Shaped Kids* certainly did. We never cease being a bit surprised, at times even amazed, when comparing the finished product with a project's original storyboard version. Somehow, along the way, it comes "alive" and a kind of birthing process unfolds. It's a mystery that we can't fully explain. But it happens—almost every time. And *Faith-Shaped Kids* has been no exception to this.

However, let us be very clear; this book did *not* complete itself. It came about as every book does—with a lot a prayer, thought, sweat, and . . . one word at a time! Plus, lots of people have been involved from the beginning to make this project happen. Most of them we've already thanked personally. But let the record show that the following players hold a special place in our hearts for their key contributions.

First, Jim Bell (not a relative!), acquisitions and product development manager at Moody Press, for his unrelenting persistence and prodding—almost two years worth—which we needed before we felt compelled to tackle this project. *Does the world really need another book on parenting?* we hesitatingly wondered upfront. Eventually, however, we sensed a leading from the Lord that it was the right thing to do. Jim, your patience and encouragement were invaluable in this process. Thanks so much.

Second, gratitude and recognition are due to Jim Vincent, our exceptional editor. He really helped us make this book better! Jim, we're particularly thankful for your support and our developing and deepening trust relationship with you as well as with the larger Moody Press team. All of you represent a "well-oiled machine" with remarkably skilled people who are unique gifts to the cause of Christ and His kingdom. We especially want to thank: Anne Scherich, Michele Straubel, Pamela Pugh, and Amy Peterson.

In addition, we are grateful to John Hinkley, director of marketing; Dave DeWit, director of editorial; and Greg Thornton, publisher. A big thank you also to Greg Wheatley (host of the Moody Broadcasting Network's *Primetime America*) who, enroute to and from work, willingly and joyfully served as "courier," transporting our latest editions of the various manuscript parts needed to bring this project across the finish line.

Finally, special thanks to our pastor, Bill Hybels; our brother-in-law, Daryle Doden, and a number of other friends (whose names we've changed in the text) who granted us permission to use their personal stories throughout *Faith-Shaped Kids*. Thanks for the role all of you have played not only in this book, but especially in our lives. We love each one of you. Blessings!

WHAT IS
THE BEST WAY TO
TEACH YOUR CHILD
ABOUT GOD?

Because they care, Christian parents will search just about anywhere to find the answer to such questions as "What is the best way to teach our children about God?" and "How can we help shape our children to faith?"

Looking for a foolproof system?

"We'll go to that conference!"

"Christian school? Home school? We'll try it!"

"Bible memorization? How many verses a week should they memorize?"

"A parenting system that grows them up Christian? Sign us up!"

"A guarantee for spiritualizing my children? Terrific—we're in!"

Speaking as parents who have "been there," we know the longing for assurance that we will be able to raise our children Christian. A clear-cut formula would be nice. Simply follow through on steps one, two, and three, and you'll produce spiritual kids—just like that!

If that's what you're looking for, then don't read this book.

But what we have learned during our parenting years we pass

on to you. Generally the more "fool-proofing" the promise holds, the less such guaranteed systems actually deliver.

We plainly state that there are no guarantees. As long as God honors free will, there will be no guarantees. That means Christian parents can still have children who reject the Christian faith. But even with such a scenario, parents are not impotent when it comes to their children's faith.

Far from it.

The premise of this book is that parents matter.

Parents are far more influential in a child's faith development than most realize. Parents, to an incredible extent, are the number one defining factor in a child's ability to embrace God. Parents and children are so intimately linked spiritually that you cannot talk about a child's faith without also talking about the faith of the parent. We are continually amazed at how much faith formation in children is actually a group experience; it's not something we just teach the kids, but something we all get to learn together.

The solution to the Christian parent's most pressing question, "How can I help my child believe?" is not answered primarily through a systems grid but through the relational grid. Relationship is the greatest faith-shaping tool a parent possesses. We would like to show you how to maximize this gift in order to help your child become a kid, a teenager, and a young adult who is shaped to faith.

But maximizing a parent's role in shaping a child's faith requires a certain level of "getting it" on the part of Mom or Dad. What do we mean? Well, a wise man once said, "Life is a succession of lessons that must be lived to be understood" (Ralph Waldo Emerson).

That's so true. First you get the test: with hardly any preparation or training, you are living the experience. It's only later that you "get it"—the lesson, what it was all about. So it's afterward that you're an expert on two-year-old temper tantrums—when your kids are four! It's only afterward that you know how to help with homework in a way that's truly productive, and by the time you excel at it, they've graduated from college! It's afterward that you're full of advice about dating—when all of your kids are finally married.

If this is true of rearing kids to become responsible and mature adults, it's equally true of parenting your children's faith. To excel at parenting children spiritually requires a higher level of "getting it" while you're experiencing it than any other aspect of parenting. That's because the optimum faith-growing condition for children to mature spiritually is having parents who "get it," not just later but *during* the experience. *Spiritually aware parents help a child shape to faith more than any other factor.*

But no one begins as an expert. Learning to parent the souls of our children was the learning-curve ride of our lives! No matter how much Valerie and I anticipated becoming parents, we found we were never quite prepared for this aspect of our job. When "kids happened," instead of feeling competent and ready, we felt like we were just hanging on.

Most of the books and available advice on parenting had expertise in helping us meet the physical, social, intellectual, and emotional needs of our kids. But a need for a certain kind of significant help still went unaddressed. We never received anything close to a map of the pathways of a child's soul. Where were the descriptions of the unique characteristics of children's spirituality? Where were the explanations of our role as parents in our kids' spiritual formation? What signs should we be looking for? When should we pray? What conditions created optimal spiritual growth? What did our kids need spiritually? Could they get this from us? Who could help us understand the spiritual dynamic between our kids and ourselves?

We needed some help to "get it."

We are empty nesters these days. We are mostly in the afterward stage of parenting. We now understand some of the things we didn't "get" while we were going through it. We're hoping we can help you to excel while you're still "taking the test." We want to share the lessons we've learned along the way about how faith forms in a child's life.

We have been down this road already. Or rather we should say, we have taken this roller-coaster ride before you. We have dangled over the precipice, been whipped around, and turned upside down and inside out. We have hung on, white-knuckled, eyes screwed shut, mouth open in silent delight or terror—we weren't always sure which. During the ride, our "hands on" parenting years, we just tried to survive. But now that it's over, not only has the world stopped spinning and our stomachs settled, we are also understanding it better. We can evaluate it enough to say, "Wow. Wasn't that something? That was a real learning curve. What a lesson!"

We are still learning. Perhaps the most impacting truth is this: faith formation in kids is never just about the kids. Parents, for better or worse, are joined to their children at the faith hip. One's growth stimulates the other. One's pain hurts the other. We intimately travel the faith journey together. But whether or not children get much out of the trip depends on how skilled their parents are at pointing out the markers, how expertly they recognize the signs of the ways God works, and whether their own strength holds strong when the trip becomes frightening.

We have something different to say to parents. It is this: you parent the soul of a child. If faith formation in your child is more than a subplot to you, if it is more than a subtitle to "more important" parental themes, if the shape of your child's soul is a primary concern for you, then you are just the parent for whom this book is written.

We wish we could have read this book, or one like it, when we were beginning our own parenting journey. And we wish we knew then what we know now. The nine lessons that follow are not a formula for assured success but are truths that can impact your kids' lives and make a difference in how you live as parents. And the four articles that conclude the book include some of the practical resources that may well serve you and your family.

An important note: In the chapters that follow, sometimes we refer to *parents* (plural), and at other times we'll say *parent* (singular). In most instances, what's being said applies in both two-parent and single-parent situations. Be quick to personalize what's being said to fit your particular circumstances.

One final note: If you are distanced from your child for any reason, or if you're concerned that irreparable damage has already been caused to your child's soul, please remember that God also parents our children and that He always writes the final chapter. With God, anything can happen. It is not our intent to load you down with guilt-producing information in the "Oh, no—I didn't get it!" department. Our hope is that you will be comforted and your load lightened by the knowledge that God is closer, more caring, and much more involved in your children's lives than you may have understood before.

Enough of introductory comments. It's time to buckle up. Harness yourself into your seat. The ride begins in the time it takes to turn this page.

These are the lessons we learned along the way.

And I will pour out my Spirit and my blessings on your children. They shall thrive like watered grass, like willows on a river bank. "I am the Lord's," they'll proudly say . . . and tattoo upon their hands the name of God.

. . . .

—ISAIAH 44:3–5 (TLB)

1

Lesson One

FAITH *IS* THE GREATEST LIFE ADVANTAGE

To be a parent is to know about hopes and dreams. Just watch the parents of any newborn. That doughy, diapered baby-body is barely home from the hospital before Mom and Dad are discovering evidences of genius intelligence or prodigious musical talent or some other sign that their child is exceptional.

"Did you see how he smacked that ball? What an eye for a two-year-old. Hey! Hey! Hey! Sammy Sosa, you're history."

"She colors all day long! Her color palette is reminiscent of Monet. Maybe we should get her into the three-year-old art classes at the community center. No, that might hold her back. We'd better look into private lessons to maximize her giftedness."

Parents are to be forgiven for such inflated ideas. After all, it's natural for us to want great lives for our children. And so we look for signs of giftedness—genius IQ, athletic prowess, ease in making friends, a quick wit, the ability to articulate, stunning beauty that launches ships, or a special moneymaking bent—something unique or outstanding that will help our children in life. Then, when promise peeks out from their early years, we eagerly invest our financial resources and energy into their potential. What family hasn't organized its schedule around sports activities, art or music lessons, speech team, or drama practices and performances? Who hasn't watched (or maybe even occasionally experienced) a passion for a child's having a leg up in life that turns normally sane adults into aggressive sports maniacs or pushy backstage moms or dads?

Our daughter-in-law, Kailey, teaches extracurricular music lessons in preschools. She has told us that after only a month or two of lessons, some parents ask, "Is my child musically gifted?" Then, if they suspect that the child is not *outstandingly* gifted, it is not uncommon for them to withdraw him from music lessons and enroll him in another type of class where he *might* be "discovered" as exceptionally gifted. And most of these children are just two- and three-year-olds!

If you and I are honest, we'd admit that we understand this strong desire. We've felt that pull with our own kids. It seems that dreaming ambitious dreams for our children is a major drive, an inescapable parental force. After all, what is better than having a dream for a child come true?

We have a friend we'll call Jack who has worked at hard manual labor all his life. His life story is told in his handshake—straightforward, callused, and bone-crushing strong. But lately Jack has been living a dream through the life of his son. His son, Tim, is a gifted baseball pitcher and honor roll student. During Tim's senior year in high school, he received an appointment to the United States Military Academy at West Point. But the father's dream was only beginning. In the spring of his senior year, Jack's son was also drafted by a professional baseball team, with a signing bonus of $150,000—enough money to attend college anywhere when Tim's baseball days are through.

What a trip! Jack is seeing his hopes and dreams for his child come true beyond his wildest imagination.

IS MY CHILD GIFTED?

Why do we want so much for our children? Maybe at the heart of all this hope is the strong desire for our children to have better lives than our own. We resonate with such dreams because we are typical parents—wanting more for our children than we had in our own lives. And so, through the years, Valerie and I have held this kind of "blessing vigil" over the emerging lives of our own two sons—a time of watching and recognizing their talents, all of which are gifts from God.

As we write, beside us on the desk is evidence of "giftedness" from our oldest son's childhood. It still amazes us. During the opening week of a summer sculpting class, Brendan, only seven at the time, fashioned his first sculpture from tinfoil. Two soccer players stand poised to kick a ball. Right legs are raised and extended behind the bodies for optimum power kicks; arms balance the perfectly proportioned aluminum bodies. Though we are adults, we could not have captured that moment half as well as our young son. *Where did this come from? Not from us.* Our proud hearts proclaimed, *Aha . . . So that's what this child is about! A sculptor. He's more gifted than we are. How amazing! How wonderful.*

"Hey! Hey! Hey! Rodin, you're history."

It was our first clue about the uniqueness of this son.

We also glowed with pride when our second son, Justin, walked on a stage for the first time and sang with all the confidence of a seasoned adult. *Stage presence! You can't take your eyes off him. He's a natural. So that's what this child is about. A performer. Where did that come from? He's more gifted than we are. How amazing! How wonderful.*

"Hey! Hey! Hey! Brad Pitt can't even sing."

Parents delight in their first discoveries about the potential of a child. It's as if a wonderful stranger has been living in their house and they are getting to know him or her. *She's balanced and steady. Maybe it's a sign of a high emotional IQ. He has lots of friends. Everyone loves him. Maybe some relational genius is starting to show.*

THE BEST KIND OF GIFTEDNESS

But of all the dreams Valerie and I have held for our children, through the years we have become more convinced of the importance of one dream above all others—that our child be gifted in faith. *No parental passion is more worthy for any parent's child than that the child should be gifted in faith.*

Faith? Why faith? Because no other life blessing is more crucial and determinative. Next to faith, all other blessings pale. Faith is life's most outstanding asset. It gives the greatest leg up in life.

Yes, faith is life's greatest advantage. Why? Because faith boosts other giftedness to supernatural levels. Faith sustains life—it is the food of the soul. A child shaped to faith is a child who is greatly blessed!

The farther down the parental path we travel, the stronger the hidden truth about faith emerges. Faith makes an incredible difference in a life. A trusting relationship with God is life's greatest treasure.

If you are tempted to shrug that off as merely "God talk," look for a moment at some of the most commonly desired dreams parents hold for their children and measure them next to the remarkable benefits of faith.

For instance, think about intellectual giftedness. That's high on the what-we-want-for-our-kids list of most parents. What parent hasn't dreamed that his or her child would be brilliant in some area—smart enough to win a full-ride scholarship before the college bills start flooding in? After all, brains do give a kid a major leg up in life.

But this highly desired gift of human intelligence is also potentially limited. Without God's influence on your children, their intelligence is just brain cells—sometimes poorly used, misused, or not used at all. There is a spiritual component to intelligence that is far more than brain cells: *inspiration*. This factor often makes the difference between someone who is just a card-carrying member of Mensa (scoring in the top 2 percent of IQ and verifying sheer brilliance) and someone whose genius is inspired to labor and sacrifice on a focused cause that will change the world for the better. High IQ without the ability to tap into God's wisdom is a highly limited resource—one that always falls far short of its world-impacting promise.

Another perceived advantage-in-life category that parents commonly pursue passionately is athletics. Certainly most of us feel parental pride over a kid with a great soccer leg, a dead-aim basketball shot, or lightning speed that's an advantage in almost any sport—right? That's great! We don't want to pop this bubble for anyone. As a dad and former "jock" myself, I really understand this one. But while you're basking in the glow in the stands at the high school football games or reading all about the sports star with your last name in the local paper's sports section, consider this. Athletic ability is merely superior coordination unless it is joined by courage.

It is courage, which comes from deep within, that presses a talented body beyond physical endurance to the "impossible win."

What makes the difference between a talented quitter and a world-class athlete? It's courage, tenacity, and endurance—all inner qualities of God-given strength. When tapped into, they take human potential to a whole new level. There's a very real spiritual dimension to these interior qualities.

Athletic ability and a well-trained body are great gifts. But don't overlook the importance of having a spiritual edge as well—the ability for your children "who hope in the LORD [to] renew their strength. They will soar on wings like eagles; they will run and not grow weary, they will walk and not be faint" (Isaiah 40:31). In life, it's often faith—that spiritual edge—that achieves the impossible win.

Here's a different parental perk for some moms and dads: a child who stops traffic with his or her good looks. Do people catch their breath and frequently remark, "What a gorgeous child!" Are you thinking beauty pageants and college scholarships? Well, the world loves a beautiful face, but consider that without faith, when outer beauty fades, all may seem lost. How much better to hope for a beautifully souled child—one who shines with the character of God, a child whose adult loveliness could never be compromised by aging or wrinkles. What a difference faith makes in all the giftedness areas of life!

How about this one? Anybody have a kid who can make, save, and turn a buck? Dreaming about early retirement funded by your little financial genius? Then think for a moment about life on easy street. Even the resources of great wealth stand powerless to buy the most precious life commodities of love and contentment and belonging—all outgrowths of the spirit and soul. We are utterly convinced that a secular life, even one with great privilege, is the most underprivileged life of all. Secular thinking reduces life to the cold, hard facts of cause and effect. Mystery and miracle cease to be. Awe and wonder are topics left unexplored in secular conversation.

Life without faith is bleak. You can have all the financial advantages this world can offer, but without faith, you are life challenged—as impoverished in soul as any homeless person is lacking materially while living on the streets. Spiritually neglected children suffer a serious form of impoverishment regardless of their material blessings. The long-range implications may be more damaging than any other form of neglect a child can suffer.

A PARENT'S BEST DREAM

A kid shaped to faith is a parent's best dream. Think about it: faith boosts all other life blessings to new levels. A parent with a child shaped to faith discovers a tremendous return on that investment—for a lifetime! If the truth would get out, if our parenting culture actually grasped the benefits of faith, more and more moms and dads would be signing up their kids for lessons in it as soon as they could. Parents would be demanding extracurricular nursery school classes, hoping to discover *spiritual* giftedness in their children. Most of us who are parents would be seeking private tutoring in faith so our kids would excel in it. Many of us would move anywhere, invest any amount of money, sacrifice whatever would be necessary to shape our kids to faith.

Faith provides a major leg up in life. But there is more. Faith will boost other life gifts. True. But still there is more. To live life at its best, faith is as necessary as food or water. Faith sustains life.

Faith is the soul's food. Let us explain.

WHAT FAITH IS

What is faith? It is the recognition that God is with us and for us. Faith is the spotlight that shines into life's darkest moments and shows the way through the seemingly impassable abyss. "Take courage. Be optimistic," faith declares.

Faith is the interior muscle that refuses to give up even when swamped by tears and discouragement. "Keep moving. Don't quit. Don't despair," faith cheers.

Faith is life's sweetener. It is the midwife of hope, the "birther" of comfort. Faith reminds us: "There is meaning in your life. There's a holy reason to everything that happens to you. You matter to God."

Faith is the crazy courage that moves the mountain that reason declares is unmovable. Faith gives the spirit wings and the soul empowerment to believe that mystery works beyond what is apparent. "You are more than body. You are intrinsically spiritual. You are eternally precious to God," faith reminds us.

Faith is the limitless spiritual resource when human reserves are depleted. It is the smile of the Spirit, the hug of God, the knowing beyond knowing. To live a life of faith, to experience life as a friend of God is to live the most privileged life of all. Faith transforms human giftedness into something more—it introduces the resources of God into a life.

That's why Scripture describes faith as "the substance of things hoped for, the evidence of things not seen" (Hebrews 11:1 KJV). This same text is translated in the *New International Version,* "Now faith is being sure of what we hope for and certain of what we do not see." In other words, faith or trust in God is foundational to a hopeful spiritual existence. Faith is the determining gift that makes the difference between a sustained life and a depleted life. Faith supersedes and influences all other gifts life has to offer a child. That's why a faith-filled life is the worthiest dream a parent can hold for a well-loved child.

Understand, we are not talking about the kind of faith that casually tips its hat toward God, or faith as a life additive that's nice for certain older people looking for something to do; nor are we describing faith as a required belief system that is the basis for membership in a type of social club. None of these. We are talking about faith that shapes a life to God and His heart. Nothing less.

BEING SUCKED IN TO SOCIETY'S VALUES

When we first had children, like most parents, we wanted to give them the best opportunities we could afford. We eagerly sought out the wealth of advice available to parents—about nutrition, health care, helping a child mature socially, optimal intellectual development, issues that contribute to the emotional well-being of a child, and more. We read tons of books. We listened to the experts. We asked questions. We moved to the best school system we could afford. We supplemented our children's classroom education with outside lessons. We were soccer, baseball, football, gymnastics, and track and field parents.

Regularly we provided the host home for our children's friendships and many of their activities. What we were doing on behalf of our boys was comparable to what we perceived most of the other parents we knew were doing for their kids.

There was nothing wrong with those activities, of course. But in the fray of all this well-intended activity, we have to confess that at times we were distracted in our parenting process. Living in today's culture, it's sometimes frighteningly easy to be satisfied with less than the very best.

Too frequently, unwittingly, we bought in to values we didn't even hold. We needed to realign our dreams, our energies, and our passions with our real values.

Have you noticed—it's so easy to be sucked in to society's values. We were faithful churchgoers. In our family life, God was always included—mealtime prayers, bedtime Bible stories, and playing Christian music and tapes were routine in our home. Of course, we believed that faith was very important—we were in full-time ministry! But in our pursuit of life advantage for our children we were often distracted from the foundational truth that our primary assignment was to parent the souls of our children. In a heartbeat we could be sucked-in to applying parental energy to every other possible place of life advantage. Too many times, spiritual life and development were simply left to "come along for the ride."

Looking back it is somewhat painful to realize that those "Aha ... So this is what our child is about!" moments were clearly there for successes in academics, sports, and similar kinds of achievements—in music, school elections, dramatics, art shows, whatever. Our Christmas letters always celebrated "blessings" such as these. The Bell fridge was clad in magnetized clumps of report cards, photographs, and the occasional newspaper clippings. We took joy in bragging about *those* developments to any family and friends who would indulge us and receive it with happiness. But reflecting, we now realize we sometimes failed to as clearly express "Aha!" over the signs of our children's emerging spirituality.

To be honest, the spiritual indicators were too frequently lost in the pursuit of today's culture values: grades, sports, and honors tied to other more tangible achievements.

YOUR PASSIONS . . . AND YOUR KIDS' VALUES

So, what's a parent to do?

First, clarify your passions. If you hold to the conviction that faith *is* the greatest life advantage, you must set your heart toward it. If a parent does not clearly pursue this core value with the kind of parental energy that goes to other try-to-get-a-leg-up-in-life categories, then faith may be perceived by children as having little or no value in real life.

Your passions shape your kids' values. Look at your heart. What passionate messages are you giving your kids? If your strongest passion is for sports, then the little ones in your home may be convinced that there's nothing more important in life than excelling athletically.

If good grades get your most enthusiastic "thumbs up," then be aware that your kids may develop a greater inclination toward the pursuit of rationality over spirituality.

If your energy goes primarily into musical achievements, don't be surprised if the dominant beat your children hear is not the rhythm of the soul.

If conversations around your dinner table are for the most part dominated by late-breaking news concerning cars, boats, vacations, and acquiring more and more and bigger and better—don't be shocked if your children grow up to become shameless materialists.

Kids just know. They read us at a deep intuitive level. Sometimes they read our passions better than we do ourselves. Our kids read us like a book. Our younger son, a recent college graduate, is expressing his faith in so many refreshing ways at this time in his life. He challenges our thinking, continually exposing us to alternative viewpoints and new ideas. He's also remarkably articulate and can evaluate our parenting. After an honest father-son talk that revealed some of our shortcomings, I playfully asked, "Well, in light of your observations about Mom and me, how come you turned out so good? How did you avoid the potential damage along the way?" Justin's answer provided a bittersweet insight to us. "Well, you and Mom did have a few parenting gaps through the years . . . but I also knew what you *really* cared about. You were passionate about faith in God; and you really cared about me. I never questioned that."

Whew! Relief. Thankfully, our core passions were perceivable and compensated for our gaps.[1]

It seems children are intrinsically skilled at two things; happily for all of us, forgiveness is one. The other skill they seem to universally possess is the uncanny ability to clearly read their parents' passions. Say what you want, blow holy smoke to the sky, quote chapter and verse, but if passion is missing, they will sense what really matters to you. If faith is not "impassioned" by parents, a child quickly learns that spirituality is probably nothing that is worth much of a life investment, certainly not something worth the intensity of long-haul discipleship.

This is a slippery slope. We have learned to examine our hearts. What *do* we really care about? Are we honest about this? Are our passions authentically aligned with our core values? We know how easy it is to lose focus on spiritual values—to convey to our kids, even when we didn't really believe it, that other things were more earth-shatteringly important.

GOD GIVES FAITH, BUT PARENTS SHAPE IT

Once we began to understand how conveying our true passions impacted our children's faith formation, another unsettling truth about our role in our children's faith became clearer. Scripture speaks of faith as a mystery, ultimately a gift of God. Some have interpreted this truth almost passively—as if the parents are barely included in the process. This passive approach to faith formation completely misses the point. God gives faith, that's true. But parents shape it. Spiritual education in children that leads to true spiritual formation is about relationship more than curriculum. *Faith-shaped kids are developed most readily through faith-shaped parents.*

Parents, by far, play the most defining role in a child's spiritual formation. Dad or Mom matter more than peers, environment, school, church, or any other kind of formal religious education.

How parents matter in a child's faith formation is illustrated in Jesus' parable of the sower and the seed. Let's look at this parable through the family grid. Jesus' image of young seedlings and the tender care they require to grow into maturity are appropriate pictures of the early faith of a child. In this parable Jesus warns of the hazards of young faith, a faith in germination, a faith without mature spiritual rootedness—the perfect description of the faith of children in formation.

> A farmer went out to scatter seed in a field. While the farmer was scattering the seed, some of it fell along the road and was eaten by birds. Other seeds fell on thin, rocky ground and quickly started growing because the soil wasn't very deep. But when the sun came up, the plants were scorched and dried up, because they did not have enough roots. Some other seeds fell where thornbushes grew up and choked the plants. But a few seeds did fall on good ground where the plants produced a hundred or sixty or thirty times as much as was scattered. (Matthew 13:3–8 CEV)

The implications for the parent's role in a child's faith formation are noteworthy. Apparently God plants the seeds of faith freely, even in places that are not reasonable for growth. You could say He is indiscriminate, desiring that all should come to Him. As the seeds of faith are scattered, we do not need to spend one ounce of worry concerning whether God can then grow the planted faith in our child's heart. He always does His part.

But outside factors matter. Before a child's faith is rooted—while it is young, tender, and fragile—a parent's job is both to watch for those outside destructive factors and to encourage the signs of spiritual life and growth. A parent tends what is tender. God gives faith. Parents shape it.

THE SPIRITUALLY AMBITIOUS PARENT

Through the years, Valerie and I learned to look for clues about who our children were becoming. We took note of their personalities. We noticed their life preferences and tendencies. But almost as a subtext, between the lines as it were, another watch began to take place. We began to observe our children's emerging souls. In no other area did the "emerging stranger" living in each child's developing personality amaze us more. This was fascinating. A subtle shift in our energies and priorities began to take place. Faith was not just a subtitle; it began to take on a main theme in our interest in our sons' development.

To use what may seem like an odd phrase, we became "spiritually ambitious" for our children—eager for them to have and to be all that God wanted for them. What exactly that entailed, we weren't sure initially. But over time and with some intentionality, we learned what to look for. Was there evidence of life present? Was young faith struggling, wilting, or falling off? Were there signs of disease? Any invading pests? Was something thwarting or distracting them from spiritual growth? Were weeds choking out their emerging faith? Were there positive indicators of movement toward God? Was there new growth, a cutting edge learning curve in their tender young souls? Overseeing this whole process became our most joyful role—to foster what was forming spiritually. We were discovering that parenting a child's soul is both a fascinating and sacred watch.

A PARENT'S FAITH:
THE GROWTH MEDIUM FOR A CHILD'S FAITH

This book attempts to explain what we've learned about a parent's unique position in a child's spiritual life. Our point of view is that parents shape a kid's faith primarily through the relational grid—as contrasted to formalized spiritual education or any other "methodical" approach. The daily sharing of family life gives you, as a parent, access to your child's soul like no other person. If there's authentic connectedness in the home, a child will benefit immensely, often not only to the point of faith but to a special spiritual sensitivity, even a kind of rare spiritual giftedness.

Living with faith-shaped parents provides children an opportunity for exposure to God and to a more mature faith. Until children have lived through their own God-rescued moments, until they recognize the signs of God's leading and are spiritually mature, before they know how to trust God themselves, they will need to see that God is trustworthy based on the track record in their parents' lives.

The spiritual growing medium that parents of faith provide for their children is their own faith. Children, with immature root systems, grow in the garden of their parents' faith—and this day-by-day access is a tremendous advantage in life. Spiritual sensitivity in children is often directly linked to the unique relationship that a child enjoys with a faith-filled parent.

As parents, look to become spiritual opportunists, finding ways "whether you're at home or walking along the road or going to bed at night, or getting up in the morning" (Deuteronomy 11:19 CEV) to say, "This is my God. This is how you recognize Him working in your life. This is a sign He's here with us. Learn to look at life from a bigger perspective than human eyesight. Trust God."

You can learn to show your children how eternal truths can jump off the pages of Scripture into real life, how words from sermons can be especially intended for us, how God becomes a part of our daily inner dialogue through prayer. Recognize that you share a walk of faith with your children, not just a set of beliefs. It's as if we parents have a well-traveled map of the soul that we share with our children, encouraging the most fascinating journey of all—the inner journey of the human spirit toward God.

A key way to share that spiritual journey with your children is through spiritually focused family activities and special projects with them, both at home and away. The "Family Resource Articles" at the end of this book include user-friendly family tools such as "The God Hunt," and "The Sunday Search" to help your children and you on that journey.

As parents tend the souls of their children, they give from their own inner beings the spiritual nourishment that keeps faith alive. The result of all this tending and soul care will be spiritually attached children—children connected to both their physical parents and God Himself. Trust with Dad or Mom (or better yet Dad *and* Mom) more easily transfers into trust with God. Such trust can make all the difference in the seed of faith growing to maturity through whatever life dumps out—through wind and fire, pestilence and overgrowth.

Be a spiritually involved parent, and your message to "trust God" will find a receptive place in your children's hearts.

MORE THAN CHAUFFEURS

But even with the best of intentions, we parents can sometimes settle for lesser roles in our children's spiritual lives. How subtly we can become just the chauffeurs who get them to Sunday school, or the benefactors who pay the tuition for their Christian educations, or merely disengaged proponents of biblical standards, all the while being the biggest cheerleaders for every other aspect of their lives. Valerie and I understand this. We've lived there. With so many other pressing priorities and all the possibilities for spiritual "busyness," it's very easy to miss the hands-on work of shaping your children's faith—and not even noticing what's really taking root in their spiritual development.

Some children will never experience that closely connected spiritual relationship with their parents that can gift children with an intuition for God. Sadly, many of these "deprived" children will be from theologically sound "Christian" homes.

Don't misunderstand us. We honor and value Christian education in its many forms: Sunday schools, Christian day schools, church youth ministries, campus clubs, family camps, student Bible study groups. All are wonderful support resources for the believing home. Formal, concrete, cognitive learning has its place in faith formation, to be sure. But religious information must be converted to faith application in the private places of children's hearts. The information must jump off the page and into life. Typically, a parent is in the most intimate position to initiate and apply that process.

Whether a child can face life with courage, resourcefulness, tenacity, and joy often comes down to how his or her soul was parented.

EARLY SIGNS OF SPIRITUALITY

Parents can learn to read the early signs of emerging spirituality:
What's this pushing to the light? She loves to pray.

Look what's blooming here. He talks so freely to all of his friends about Jesus.

How wonderfully strong and tall she's growing toward God—singing out her heart to Him all the time.

Wow! He has more faith than we do sometimes.

Here's a tender heart of mercy forming—she wants to give all her toys to children who don't have any.

As you make discoveries like these along the way, Dad and Mom, stand up and cheer.

GARAGE OR FOREVER INVESTMENTS?

Looking back, we wish we hadn't spent a moment grieving over report cards or athletics or some of the other things in our children's lives that seemed so pressing and important. Our garage is a testament to the minimal return on some of our investments. We look at the bins and boxes that store their cast-off clothing and gear—small soccer jackets, football jerseys, baseball gloves, BMX dirt bikes—and realize that what was once hotly pursued, exciting for a season or a few years, has become just the unwanted remnants from their lives. For all the parental energy and investment in hopes and dreams our two boys received, those values are not lasting.

But think of faith! Our children—your children—can receive the greatest and most enduring of all of life's advantages—the gift of faith. Someday you will no longer have a direct role in your children's lives. Then, when your parental applause is silenced, when your cheering for them is only a remembered echo, faith will remain to comfort, guide, strengthen, and sweeten.

LIVING IN SPIRITUAL ANTICIPATION

The following prayer by Sir Francis Drake, the first Englishman to navigate the globe, captures the heart of the message we want to convey to fellow Christian parents throughout this book:

A PRAYER

Disturb us, Lord, when
We are too well pleased with ourselves
When our dreams have come true
Because we dreamed too little,
When we arrived safely
Because we sailed too close to shore.

Disturb us, Lord, when
With the abundance of things we possess
We have lost our thirst for the waters of life;
We have ceased to dream of eternity

31

And in our efforts to build a new earth,
We have allowed our vision
Of the new Heaven to dim.

Disturb us, Lord, to dare more boldly,
To venture on wider seas
Where storms will show your mastery;
Where losing sight of land,
We shall find stars.

We ask you to push back
The horizons of our hopes;
And to push us in the future
In strength, courage, hope and love.[2]
       —Sir Francis Drake
       December 1577

We invite you and your family to "get into our boat." We are going to cast off from shore and travel into what might be uncharted waters for some. We hope you will travel spiritually with us for a while and let us share what we have learned about faith-shaped kids and their faith-shaped parents.

NOTES

1. You never know when your values may sink in. One of my most cherished possessions is a letter I received from Justin on Father's Day 1999. I've actually carried it around in my briefcase for the past two years, and every couple of months will pull it out to reread and refresh my memory and soak in some of the encouragement it contains. The power of this letter ministers to a deep place in my soul and causes me to reflect on one of my all-time favorite assignments in this life—participating with Valerie in the parenting process of our two sons, Brendan and Justin.

   This letter reminds me that children are incredibly gracious and forgiving, and that "love [in the truest sense!] covers a multitude of sins." In his own handwriting Justin printed the letter in all caps. It reads:

                                                JUNE 18, 1999
       DEAR DAD,
           HAPPY FATHER'S DAY!! IS MOM BACK FROM NORTH CAROLINA YET? I WOULDN'T WANT YOU TO SPEND FATHER'S DAY WITHOUT BOTH ME AND MOM, SO I'M HOPING SHE HAS RETURNED.
           AND TODAY IS ALSO THE MARKING OF 29 YEARS OF MARRIAGE FOR YOU GUYS!! RIGHT? THAT IS AWESOME! THE MORE I GET EXPOSED TO DIFFERENT FAMILIES, MARRIAGES, AND VALUE

SYSTEMS THE MORE I REALIZE HOW RARE AND WONDERFUL OUR FAMILY LIFE IS. THERE IS NO SENSE OF JEALOUSY, RESENTMENT, OR ANGER IN OUR FAMILY. IT HAS ALWAYS BEEN SEEN AS INAPPROPRIATE BEHAVIOR AND IS NOT TOLERATED. I HAVE ONLY FELT LOVE, ACCEPTANCE, AND SUPPORT WITH YOU DAD, AND I HOPE TO GIVE THAT SAME TYPE OF HEALTHY STABILITY TO MY WIFE AND KIDS. WHEN KAILEY TELLS US HOW EASY IT IS TO LIVE WITH BRENDAN I THINK YOU AND MOM CAN CLAIM RESPONSIBILITY. YOU GUYS SET A GREAT EXAMPLE!

SPECIFICALLY, ON THIS FATHER'S DAY . . . I THANK YOU FOR ALLOWING ME TO PURSUE MY DREAMS. YOU NEVER HAVE TRIED TO TALK ME OUT OF THINGS OR FORCE ME INTO BEING SOMEONE I AM NOT. THE LOVE THAT YOU SHOW MOM, BRENDAN, KAILEY, AND MYSELF IS CHRIST-LIKE, UNSELFISH AND GENUINE. THAT IS WHY I LOVE YOU IN RETURN, BECAUSE YOU LOVED ME FIRST.

THANKS FOR BEING A GREAT DAD,
JUSTIN

Lord, I don't know what to say except thank You for our children. They are gifts, treasures from You. Enable me, God, in the days to come to learn to be the person, father, husband, and leader You want me to be—for Christ's sake.

2. As adapted in a playbill of the 2000 Canadian Stratford Festival in Stratford, Ontario.

He is my father's God—I will exalt him.

. . . .

—EXODUS 15:2c (TLB)

2

GOD–READINESS BEGINS AT HOME

Good beginnings matter. Sprinters know, as they poise at the starting block, bodies straining in anticipation of the signal, that it may be the smallest early edge that determines who wins the race. Gardeners also know that weak young seedlings make for fragile mature plants. The quality of the beginning often determines the quality of the ending.

For a child, good beginnings also matter.

As young parents, we had a sense that this was true, but we were often fuzzy in picturing what a good beginning looked like. Should we be stricter or more relaxed? Should we always hold a crying baby? Or didn't it matter that much? Should we keep our family on a strict schedule or was it OK to be more flexible? Even with the best of intentions, we were often confused.

A STUDY ON GOOD BEGINNINGS FOR CHILDREN

But now, because of a ground-breaking new study called "A Good Beginning" by the U.S. Department of Health, a new generation of parents can have a much clearer picture of what a good beginning really looks like in their children's lives.

We just wish we had had this information when we were starting our family.

The findings in this new study challenge every traditional approach to children's learning and well-being. It reports, amazingly, that good beginnings—school-readiness and life-readiness for a child—are not so much about the traditional learning of the ABCs and 1-2-3s. Rather, when it comes to later school and life success, it's *relationships* that build social and emotional competence that are much more important. But let the study speak for itself:

> The problem of school failure is taking on new urgency because it is getting worse. Forty-six percent of kindergarten teachers report that half of the children entering kindergarten have a behavioral or learning problem and one out of thirteen children fail kindergarten or first grade. Children who do not begin kindergarten socially and emotionally competent are often not successful in the early years of school—and can be plagued by behavioral, emotional, academic, and social development problems that follow them into adulthood.
>
> The crux of the report is the new knowledge that most of a child's brain gets built after birth and that it uses interactions with other people and physical contact with its surrounding world to form neural networks for emotions, thinking and learning. It is this period before school that a child is learning to learn or to avoid learning.[1]

GOOD EARLY RELATIONSHIPS
EQUAL FUTURE LIFE SUCCESS

Wow! Here is some crucial new information that is so important for parents. Children do not come into life with a set level of intelligence. A child's brain is still very much in process—it is not a done deal or a completed work. In fact, *most* of the brain is built *after* birth. The capacity for intelligence is neurally constructed through a child's interaction with his world—specifically, through relational involvement with a parent. Simply stated, *relationship* physically grows the brain!

Good beginnings are more about parenting than we ever had evidence to suspect before. The quality of a parent's connecting with a child can actually develop that child's brain to a "readiness" mode for learning. The data now verifies that parents who reward curiosity, effort, persistence, and love of learning can literally "smarten" their kids for life!

LINKING SCHOOL-READINESS AND GOD-READINESS

But what does this have to do with faith formation in children? Stay with us. There are strong implications for the spiritual formation of children implied in this study that should greatly interest any parent of faith.

Just as good beginnings impact so much of later life, good beginnings matter in the shaping of a child's faith. The same parental relationship that determines school-readiness also can determine God-readiness. In spiritual learning—as seen by the receptivity, eagerness to learn, and curiosity of a child—as in other forms of life-learning, good relational beginnings with Mom and Dad matter. The relationship between parent and child is often the defining difference between a child of faith or one who opts out. The way a parent relates to his or her child creates a kind of spiritual preparedness or "God-readiness." Whether God is eventually embraced or avoided later in life may be set in motion in the early years of childhood. In faith, as in life, a good beginning is crucial and parents are key.

THE GOOD BEGINNING DYNAMIC

To understand more fully the role of parents in faith formation, we need to examine the concept of "nurture." What does it mean to nurture faith, or to parent a child's soul? Well, to nurture a child means a parent meets the child's physical, emotional, and spiritual needs. To be a child's need-meeter is the very definition of good parenting.[2] But this is a more sacred work than most job descriptions or ground-breaking studies on parenting indicate.

We admit it: as young parents, Valerie and I felt disenchanted with some of the mundane tasks of parenting. Meeting the needs of our kids was exhausting. We even avoided our duties sometimes, hoping the other parent would carry our weight of responsibility as well as his own. But we had to learn that so much of the daily routine of child rearing that appears insignificant and ordinary—changing diapers, feeding, reading, playing, bathing—are at their core building bonds of attachment at the most basic level. Actually, there is a spiritual dynamic in every diaper change, every feeding, every game of patty-cake. Each time a need is met, however basic—whether related to preparing a meal and eating together, or giving some special attention, providing a sense of security, responding spontaneously with laughter of delight, offering timely instruction, measuring out appropriate discipline, whatever—the attachment between parent and child is strengthened.

Attachment. It could also be called *trust*. A well-cared-for child is secure knowing that "Mom and Dad get it! They understand me." Need-meeting indicates to children the degree to which Mom or Dad "buy in" to them—the level of investment the parents are willing to make on behalf of their kids. Need meeting builds a bridge to a child's soul.

It's strategically important to understand this "good beginning" dynamic, because it may make all the difference in whether your child can eagerly embrace God or, instead, will learn to avoid spirituality altogether. Contrary to what many parents believe, faith formation doesn't begin with Sunday school or memorized Scripture verses or Christian education of any other kind—the ABCs and 1-2-3s of spiritual learning. Formal spiritual training plays a role later on. That's true. But faith begins with how a child perceives Mom and Dad. Or said differently, a parent is a child's first view of God. Professor Donald Joy puts it this way: "Parents are the curriculum."

TO A CHILD, GOD LOOKS
A LOT LIKE MOM AND DAD

All day long a child is sensing, either correctly or incorrectly, what God is like from his or her experiences with Mom and Dad. This means there is tremendous significance—power even—in the mundane exchanges most parents only manage to endure. It matters how a child is put to bed at night. It counts, for better or worse, whether fears are met with empathy or belittlement. It makes a difference whether we are there and engaged or are missing-in-action, though present in body. It matters whether a child perceives that time together is cherished or merely tolerated. Potty training, picky eating (and all the other quirky expressions of childhood that can drive a parent nuts!) are loaded with relational and trust-building significance. This is the beginning of soul care in a child's life—his or her first view of God, the foundation for God-readiness, as it were.

Consider how this works. Studies indicate that children are inclined toward God. Even before they can intellectually grasp or understand God, they are sensing that He exists and what He might be like. It's important to note that this "sensing" occurs before formal religious education begins. How? The answer is quite awesome. Even before a child can say "Mommy" or "Daddy," a child is intuiting, sensing in a deep soul place, what God might be like. We are speaking of cradle and crib spirituality here. This early capacity for faith is explained by James Fowler, author of *Stages of Faith*. He describes how this "faithing" process begins with a child's first breath.

> In the interaction of parent and child not only does a bond of mutual trust and loyalty begin to develop, but already the child, albeit on a very basic level, senses the strange new environment as one that is either dependable and provident, or arbitrary and neglectful. The covenanting pattern of faith as relational becomes clearer as we reflect on what the parent or parents bring with them to the care and nurture of the child. They bring *their* way of seeing and being in the world. They bring *their* trusts and loyalties. They bring *their* fidelities—and infidelities—to other persons and to the causes, institutions, and transcending centers of value and power that constitute their lives' meanings. Long before the child can sort out clearly the values and beliefs of the parents, he or she senses a structure of meaning and begins to form nascent images . . . of the centers of value and power that animate the parents' faith. As love, attachment, and dependence bring the new one into the family, he or she begins to form a disposition of shared trust and loyalty to (or through) the family's faith ethos.[3]

That means before a child is able to sing "Jesus loves me this I know," he or she is already sensing God—a unique God, however, a God who comes through the parenting grid. Before faith is articulated or cognitively received, it is being sensed and accepted or rejected as part of the "parenting package."

That is why every child is potentially a home-faithed child; your child can be influenced toward faith by you, his parent. Before he or she is Sunday-schooled or Christian-schooled or home-schooled, before being Christian-clubbed or Christian-camped, a child is home-faithed. This parental power of influence is both incredibly wonderful (we have more influence over our children's faith formation than we ever believed possible) and awesomely frightening (we had better get it right!). Think of the phenomenal trust God has placed in all parents to represent Him well to their children.

It's inspiring and scary and marvelous all at the same time!

PERFECT PARENTS NEED NOT APPLY

But what if you're not a perfect parent? Don't worry; you don't need to be a perfect parent to be an effective one. Valerie and I have never been perfect parents. Nor have we been ideal ones. Never! Ask our kids. We've had our share of gaps throughout the years both as young parents and now as older ones. As younger parents we would have been scared to death if we had realized our children were intuiting God through our own flawed parenting process. But a look back brings some grace to bear. During that time in our lives we were also on an enormous learning curve ourselves.

There's a certain irony that during a child's earliest and most formative years, parents are in the least skilled phase of their own development. During those highly sensitive years in our children's lives, Valerie and I often marched around in combat boots as it were, shouting orders, making things a bigger mess than they were before we got involved. The two of us were such parental neophytes! It's almost unthinkable that, by divine design, the inexperienced are entrusted to oversee such a tender impressionable era in children's lives. But in God's plan that's how it works. Young adults have young children, and everyone has a lot to learn.

We observed that in God's great plan, quite often, the learning curve or spiritual growth most needed was for us, the parents. We weren't just in the process of discovering how to raise our kids; during those rookie years, we were getting to know ourselves more honestly, discovering our own human potential—both wonderful and rotten. What parents haven't seen their best and worst selves reflected back to them through their children's eyes? It can't be denied; parenting is a reality check to the max!

During our children's early childhood years—those years so determinate to their future life success—we were exhausted most of the time, and occasionally more frustrated than we had ever experienced before. That may be how you have been, along with feeling frightened, depleted, worried, stymied, and sometimes stretched beyond anything you ever imagined by the job of caring for babies and toddlers. (And people on this kind of learning curve are not a very pretty sight!) No wonder you and I lose our tempers and our patience, not to mention our dignity. We don't enjoy our kids as much as they deserve because one day with a two-year-old can feel like an eternity. Sometimes the only thing that keeps you going is the thought of getting away from them for a few days. Us too!

Does that sound like perfect parenting, like God would do it? No? That's OK, because God uses imperfect parents. God has designed His relational wiring system to work *with*—and *on* and mostly *for*—imperfect parents. Even imperfect parents, engaged in the most basic daily need meeting, doing that which seems so mundane, reap an enormous return on their investment.

If the phrase "love covers over a multitude of sins" (1 Peter 4:8) applies to any relationship, it is especially relevant to the way the love of a child covers the mistakes of his or her parents. Well-cared-for children of imperfect parents develop attached relationships to their parents and positive results follow. Look at some of the benefits of meeting needs and creating attachments with your children.

- Children who feel attached to their parents need less discipline because they are a part of a cooperative parent-child team that is sharing a value system. Parents who meet a child's needs create trust within the child, which grows into obedience because of a desire to honor Mom and Dad. That means you don't always have to be bigger, or even be there in the same room waving a spanking spoon to get a kid to obey. You just need a child who trusts you enough to honor your values. That makes parenting much easier and far more enjoyable.

• Attached children are strengthened to face life's obstacles. Because Dad and Mom have consistently communicated "We believe in you. You can do it!" these children are more confident, quite self-assured, and courageous beyond their age in the face of adversity.

• Attached children have a powerful life model for giving and receiving love. You could say they are relationally astute (a characteristic, by the way, largely lacking in children in the national reports on school-readiness). These children have a "learned" empathy from their parents and offer it to their own worlds at early stages in their personal development.

• Attached children have a special protection from peer pressure. It's as if these kids carry Mom and Dad in their hearts whenever the heat gets turned on by a friend. Then there you are whispering and *being heard* in your children's ears at all times.

• The latest research, like the Department of Health's "A Good Beginning" study, indicates that emotionally positive relating with Mom and Dad in the early years of life may actually make children's brains more neurally developed—in other words, smarter. And on and on. The list of the benefits of attachment is endless.

TRUST WITH MOM AND DAD
BECOMES TRUST WITH GOD

But of all the advantages enjoyed by attached parents and children, the greatest by far is the clear and attractive view of God presented in the home. God has entrusted parents with this early view of what He might be like as an incredibly strong tool for soul care. Spiritual sensitivity in children—high spiritual receptivity and an inclination toward God are often the outcome.

So the answers to the pressing questions asked by parents of faith,

"How can I help my child believe?" or "What does this child need spiritually?" can be discovered, initially, by taking a look at the relational beginnings. What does that specifically look like? It's the home environment fostering a relationship between parent and child that accurately reflects the relationship between God and His children.

DO WE REFLECT GOD?

Look closely at how God parents His children. God is neither neglectful nor authoritarian but "authoritative." To use family systems language, He relates to His children with a high level of relational attachment. He is accessible to the deepest parts of our emotional beings. He has standards, but they are attainable and have a positive impact on the quality of our lives. God desires to be known and better known and expresses delight with those who walk with Him. Does this sound like the kind of parenting you are learning to give your children?

Live intimately with God and you will know what it means to live life with spiritual expectancy: "Ah, there He is again!" God often "pops off the pages" of Scripture and into the lives of those who walk with Him. Life with a parent who is in real relationship with this kind of God makes spirituality winsome, attractive, and extremely appealing.

Dallas Willard, a professor and author, describes a God of joyful capacity. To begin with, we should "think that God leads a very interesting life, and that he is full of joy. Undoubtedly, he is the most joyous being in the universe. The abundance of his love and generosity is inseparable from his infinite joy. All of the good and beautiful things from which we occasionally drink tiny droplets of soul-exhilarating joy, God continuously experiences in all their breadth and depth and richness."[4]

In other words, God is fully and joyfully alive!

Ask yourself, *Am I fully and joyfully alive?* You can learn to pump some joy into the less than spectacular, repetitious, and routine parts of family life. It can begin early; laugh and play games when the diapers are changed. Meet your children's needs without resentment. In fact, at times receive those little sleep interrupters with a comforting tuck into your bed. Try to be at least as much fun as any other parents your kids know.

With the passing of time you can learn to relax and laugh more. Express openly the joy you have in your children's activities, projects, and ideas. And do your best not to fill their emotional tanks with nonstop instructions and criticism and anxiety-producing interactions.

A LESSON IN GOD-READINESS

When you and I show such joy around our kids, we are displaying a lesson about God—really, we're intuiting a lesson in God-readiness. The optimum faith-growing medium for children is a relationship with Mom and Dad that accurately reflects who God is.

Now, you may have noticed, the picture we're describing has changed focus somewhat. Faith formation is not just about the kids anymore. Here is a piece of creative God-breathed genius at work. Wouldn't it be fair to admit that we parents would prefer an optimum faith-growing method that left us out of the picture—one where the focus is primarily on the child's faith development? A cognitive, one-way, I've-already-arrived-because-I'm-an-adult-Christian approach is one born out of a false sense of superiority. *"We're already Christians, so let's work on the kids so they don't grow up to be barbarians!"*

But God is not through with us parents yet. God's plan for our child's soul includes some continued spiritual growth for us as well. That's why He designed parents, for joy or pain, to be intimately spiritually linked with their children. Becoming a parent will be the most soul-motivating job any of us has ever taken on. We are aware of the fragile trust that exists, how easily we wound in our powerful position as parent, how unknowingly we can do damage. As never before we will need to tend our own souls for such malignancies as selfishness, pride, anger, and envy—malignancies that would compromise our children's ability to clearly receive the picture of God as a loving parent.

It's pure, raw genius the way God's family system works.

As our children's first view of God, as the precursor relationship for God-readiness, parents are to be fully and joyfully alive. Here is permission to laugh, to enjoy, to drink in life in all its wonder and power and elaborate beauty.

DISTORTED MIRRORS . . . OR A TRUE PICTURE?

Have you ever been in a house of mirrors? The mirrors are bent and twisted with dimpled curves. The images they reflect back are distorted, not a true picture. So it is with parenting a child's soul. We reflect reality about God or we reflect distortion.

As we watch the interaction between parents and children, we often wonder what picture of God a child is receiving. On a recent trip to Israel, Valerie and I were touring Jerusalem and happened upon the religious education of young Hasidic Jewish boys being tutored in their faith at the Wailing, or Western, Wall. To our Western Christian eyes, their young shoulders seemed too small for the stern indoctrination they were receiving. Draped head to shoulder in black, hair worn in dreadlocks, holding their prayer books over their faces, they rocked their bodies back and forth to a self-accompaniment of mournful sounds.

Even given the best-case scenarios—that these boys were from warm, nurturing homes—we wondered what such an approach would teach them about God. Would they see Him as a warm, tender father? Would they be able to fathom that God delights in them and loves them with unqualified love? Could they picture Him laughing at what He created and enjoying themselves with Him for all eternity?

Or would their parents' theology distort their view of a loving God? It's a revealing and fascinating connection. Look at how a parent approaches his child's spirituality and you will learn a lot about that parent's God. If you serve a demanding, perfectionistic God, then your relationship with your children—including how you approach their spiritual growth—may be marked by excessive control and domineering power instead of safe intimacy and extended grace. No wonder some children develop spiritual gag reflexes after years of being force-fed their parents' God!

We recently visited the Cherry Hill Center in a Chicago suburb, where our son Brendan works as a professional counselor. On the waiting room bulletin board, we found the following anonymous quotation. We can't help but wonder what a difference it could make for all children everywhere were they to receive, through the parenting grid, this message about God:

> I am God's child. God created me and He loves me. I was with God before I came into being. He knew me then and He knows me now perfectly. He knows me through and through. God loves me just the way I am right now. God accepts me just the way I am. I am acceptable and loveable. I am a beautiful child of God. I have infinite worth. All of creation is incomplete without me. I have been created individually. I am unique in all ways. God created me as that unique person and He loves me. God chose me as His own. God lives in me and I live in Him. He abides in me and calls me His child. He wants me to live fully and abundantly. He frees me and gives me joy. God gives me the gift of life through His grace alone. I accept God's love this day and know He will love me forever. I thank God for the real person I am. I thank Him for creating me and giving me life. I thank Him for truth and love and life.

Children with that kind of clear, undistorted early view of God will be shaping to faith before they are out of their cradles and their cribs. But that's not all. God-readiness in a child has a farther reach, influence, and implication. God-readiness is not just about producing faith-shaped kids. God-readiness leads to faith-shaped teenagers, faith-shaped young adults, faith-shaped parents, and faith-shaped grandparents. As in the rest of life, good beginnings make for good endings. And when it comes to faith, good beginnings become lifetimes of receptivity to God and openness to spiritual life.

Good beginnings matter.

Forever.

NOTES

1. Ronald Kotulak, "People Skills, Not ABCs, Aid Kindergartners, Experts Say," *Chicago Tribune,* 6 September 2000, sec. 1, p. 1.
2. Valerie Bell, *Getting Out of Your Kids' Faces and into Their Hearts* (Grand Rapids: Zondervan, 1994).
3. James Fowler, *The Stages of Faith* (New York: Harper & Row, 1981), 16–17.
4. Dallas Willard, *The Divine Conspiracy: Rediscovering Our Hidden Life in God.* (San Francisco: Harper, 1998), 62.

The praises of our fathers surrounded your throne; they trusted you and you delivered them. . . . You took me safely from my mother's womb and brought me through the years of infancy. I have depended upon you since birth; you have always been my God.

. . . .

—PSALM 22:4, 9–11a (TLB)

THERE IS NO SUCH THING AS TOO YOUNG FOR GOD

W e weren't parents very long until we realized that somewhere in each of our children was a place where parents
just couldn't go. We had to face reality that even with our
best parental efforts, there were some tears we could not dry, some
fears we could not soothe, certain strange anxieties we could not calm,
and those occasional nightmares that filled their sleep with night
terrors. Where was this all coming from? Could our very young children be that troubled already?

We were puzzled. *Is there a special parental skill missing in us?* We
asked ourselves, *Have we overlooked a critical area of development? Are
we doing something wrong?*

How stubbornly we clung to that mother of all parental fantasies
—the unspoken hope that our children's early lives would be mostly
about untroubled innocence. We wanted to believe that under our
"excellent," careful watch, they would be untouched by anything that
might be difficult.

But eventually we had to face the truth about our children's essential humanness. Very early they demonstrated needs that went far beyond food, shelter, and the desire for belonging and acceptance. These babies were far more than adorable, cuddly, innocent bodies with sweet little personalities. They were also spiritual beings—already! We were never flippant or careless about our kids' spiritual needs; we just didn't realize how early their spiritual neediness would surface in their lives.

When parents who are interested in their children's spiritual formation begin asking, "What does this child need spiritually?" it soon becomes apparent that there is a wealth of answers, for spirituality is a topic that is multifaceted, with a fluid and growing capacity. We were amazed to realize that spiritual life, even for young children, is incredibly rich and more capable of depth than we had supposed. We also became focused in our understanding that though our children needed Bible stories, bedtime prayers, and Sunday school—and yes, they needed us—more importantly, our children needed God. Children have an almost unbelievably large capacity for God—born out of some place in the soul that God alone can touch.

When we accepted that there are places in the soul where a parent cannot go, we were ready to also accept that God alone could meet those kinds of needs in our children's lives.

IS BABY FAITH REAL FAITH?

But you don't have to look very far to realize there is a lot of prejudice against baby faith. Baby faith, while incomplete, may still be an adequate understanding of God, a simple trust but genuine faith that can comfort and soothe a child. Many adults struggle to accept that it could be necessary, let alone authentic. Recently I (Valerie) was sharing coming-to-faith stories with an adult-converted woman. The "before and after" of the other woman's conversion was extremely dramatic, and it altered both her thinking and lifestyle. It was a thrilling testimony to God's redemptive grace in her heart and life.

But when it was my turn to share my story about coming to faith as a young child, I braced myself for the typical response. When I finished, the other woman maintained an awkward silence. I sensed she was processing my coming to God and was slightly dissatisfied with what she had heard.

Finally she asked, "Valerie, do you ever mind that you came to Jesus as a three-year-old?" Her question expressed what I had seen on other listeners' faces. It implies that perhaps it is best to let your adult self decide such life-impacting issues. After all, is baby faith real faith?

It is a fortunate child whose parent understands the workings of a child's soul. I was just such a child. My mother held firmly to a conviction that children, like adults, have strong, pressing, fundamental needs for a trusting relationship with God that leads to salvation, quality of life, and a spiritual walk that is transforming. So she let a three-year-old make this life-impacting decision, and I have stuck with it ever since!

"No," I told the woman, " I have no regrets. It was my very best life decision."

I was a Jesus baby.

HOW EARLY FEAR BECAME EARLY FAITH

I am quick to add that I was not a child given to "goodness," nor was I spiritually precocious. Instead, I was already a handful, a challenging piece of work! My family nickname, "Valerie B-Bomb Beth Burton," accurately captured my toddler personality, as did a poem my mother wrote about me at this age:

> "I OFTEN THINK OF VALERIE AT TWO"
> I often think of Valerie at two
> when "don't do this" and
> "don't do that"
> meant: "Do!"
>
> On counter and on windowsill
> she often tried her fledgling will—
> knew no subsequential fear
> though warned by parent, peer.
>
> When on some catwalk's edge I lean
> and risk some slough's dark algae-green,
> do Your arms stretch toward me
> as mine once did for Valerie?

Unbridled yet—my human will—
be Thou, O God, my Codicil.[1]

No, not only was I not a spiritual child, I was not even a very good little girl. I remember many off-the-wall incidents that were part of this era. I had a dangerous love of climbing to high places. Ladders left unattended, car roofs, treetops—all were invitations to me for perilous upward mobility. I enjoyed living on the edge of my parents' boundaries—to me, the lines they drew were always challenges over which to dangle a foot. Matches fascinated me, as did scissors. I distinctly remember cutting what little hair I had and throwing the remains to the wind outdoors thinking my mother would never know. Fat chance. She was distraught.

I explored the neighborhood, begging our neighbors for food, embarrassing my mother. Lying about almost everything, I decorated the stairwell with piles of soap detergent and "sweetened" the goldfish bowl with perfume—killing all of the living creatures within—while unflinchingly maintaining my innocence. Well, you get the picture.

But even with this reckless wiring, a new reality entered my life. It changed me from fearless to fearful almost overnight. A dearly loved uncle suddenly died. Never had I experienced anything like my parents' grieving. Now, prematurely, they tried to explain death to me. They talked about heaven, about God. But very quickly, instead of believing in God, I became a believer in something dark that wanted all of us. Bedtime, with its swallowing aloneness and blackness, brought my shadow faith to the surface. We were all dying. Baby bravado evaporated. I became terribly anxious and disturbed.

My mother employed the normal methods of comfort—a nightlight, a cuddly stuffed animal, a quilt pieced together from former clothing of the women in our family, a prayer—but all the traditional bedtime rituals failed to charm.

Now I lay me down to sleep
I pray the Lord my soul to keep
If I should *die* before I wake ...

What? This was comfort? Prayers about death? What was she thinking?

Nothing worked to make me feel connected and safe. Not even my mother's presence. Every night my body tensed in the dark, waiting for something unseen to consume us, until eventually, exhausted and tearful, I fell asleep. The next night the pattern was repeated with the same intensity.

Fortunately, after all human attempts had failed, my mother recognized a spiritual battle when she was in one. That was how I came, on this particular night, to be introduced to the somersaulting, mystic, joyous, word-expressive, seemingly unshakable faith of my mother. That night, for the first of many times during my growing-up years, I would borrow her faith and we would share her God.

On that particular night she once again entered my bedroom, wafting her normal nighttime smells of Ivory Soap, Pond's cold cream, and White Shoulders cologne behind her. But this would be a "no crutches" night. There would be no night-light left on, no door cracked open a sliver, and no lingering maternal presence.

Instead she directed, "Valerie, I want you to say these verses after me. These are God's promises. I use them myself when I am sad or afraid." By the way, Mother was the adult child of an alcoholic parent, a woman who as a teenager had supported her family when her own father died so very young. This was a woman who knew about fear and sadness and stressful times.

"Repeat after me," she urged.

"Let not your heart be troubled: ye believe in God, believe also in me. In my Father's house are many mansions. . . . I go to prepare a place for you . . . that where I am, there ye may be also" (John 14:1–3 KJV).

"Do you know what that means, Valerie? It means that Jesus will never leave you. He's so wonderful. And even if you were to die, Jesus would take you to heaven to be with God, and nothing could be better. We do not need to be afraid."

She made me repeat the verses until she was sure I had memorized them. Then she announced her new tactic. "I am going back to sleep. When you are afraid, say these verses and remember that Jesus is with you."

Right! This was not what I wanted. I wanted her to get into bed with me and tell me that it was all a big misunderstanding, that we weren't going to die, that there was nothing to be afraid of. Instead, she told me the terrible truth. She admitted it. Like that would solve anything. And she left me. She left me alone in the dark with her faith as my only comfort.

For several nights this routine was repeated. She refused my requests for a light to be left on in the hallway or my bedroom door to be left open a crack. There would be no little props for a child who needed a big dose of God's love. I had only her voice as a spiritual lifeline.

She continued this practice. "Here are some more verses. Repeat them after me."

"The Lord is my shepherd; I shall not want. He maketh me to lie down in green pastures: he leadeth me beside the still waters. He restoreth my soul. . . . Yea, though I walk through the valley of the shadow of death, I will fear no evil: for thou art with me; thy rod and thy staff they comfort me" (Psalm 23:1–4 KJV).

When I could say them, she left me. She left me with her God and her faith.

In time I found comfort in the words. I felt the strength of my mother's faith. Somehow the words held a power I didn't even understand.

My mother has been dead for almost twenty years now, and though she's gone, her faith and admonition to trust God remain. It was, and is, her ultimate comfort and lasting legacy. In time, I got over my nighttime terrors, but I have never in my entire lifetime gotten over my mother's faith. When I am pressed by adult worries and anxieties, sad or lonely, I am still comforted when I remember those words—I can still hear her voice: "Let not your heart be troubled. You believe in God, believe also in me."

PARENTS WHO DIGNIFY
A CHILD'S SPIRITUAL NEEDS

A child's soul and spiritual crises need to be primary concerns of parents. As parents we have a natural near obsession about our children's development. Are they growing? Are they well? Are they learning? But are we aware that our children's souls need that same kind of care? As young parents we could be very troubled when our children were in crisis, but as we became more aware of how the soul works, we began to view crisis as spiritual opportunity.

When a child hurts, it is important that parents dignify a child's evolving spirituality by recognizing that even the small heart of a child can harbor dark places that need to be healed by God. A child needs parents who respect his or her spiritual needs.

When we read what some experts prescribe for children's fears these days—everything from making light of fears with spray bottles filled with water and labeled "Monster Spray" to be spritzed around a child's bedroom, to the bald and discomforting truth that "death is natural"—we are appalled.

I am grateful my mother took my fears seriously. I am grateful for my mother's faith. At first I only borrowed it, repeating and grasping the words of faith like a remnant of my mother. But soon that borrowed faith began to take root in my toddler soul. Baby faith, a simple but genuine faith in Jesus, became the first step away from what undoubtedly could have become a life rooted in anxiety and fear. Instead, baby faith started me on a lifetime path of spiritual well-being and trust in God. I think of it as early and necessary intervention. Baby faith held firm in my life. I heard "Let not your heart be troubled . . ." at both my parents' graves. When storms of heartbreak and failure threatened to overwhelm me, those words strengthened me. When I struggled with my own cancer diagnosis just a few years after my mother's death, her faith—now my faith—comforted me.

Baby faith should never be underestimated. In the end, if we are truthful about our human condition, it really is all any of us has—the faith of a frightened child beating to the pulse of an adult body!

IT'S NEVER TO EARLY TO MEET GOD

In light of all the new information about the importance of a child's early emotional life, it seems to us that it is never too early to be introduced to real faith in God. Only by minimizing a child's deeply profound spiritual needs could we minimize or withhold this remedy of faith. The cutting-edge research about child development all points to early learning as being more developmentally formative than we have ever realized. These profound new discoveries present evidence that is compelling: brain cells begin learning *during fetal development*. Babies are capable of learning and experiencing emotions at a deeper level than we ever realized before.

As a science writer for the *Chicago Tribune* recently reported, "We now know that immediately after birth, for example, a baby can recognize the mother's voice, and even the music she listened to during pregnancy and that by the age of four months babies can experience depression."[2]

But do parents get this? Interestingly, parents surveyed in a study called "What Grown-Ups Understand about Child Development" seem misinformed of the potentialities of these early years in a child's life.[3] When asked, "At what age to you think an infant or young child begins to take in and react to the world around them?" seventy-five percent of parents of children three years old or younger gave the wrong answer—with most saying that babies don't react to their world until they are at least three months, or even a year old.

The survey found that many parents err by emphasizing flash cards, educational TV, and computer time at the expense of play (relational play), which is important for a child to build social skills and language and master important intellectual concepts and thinking capabilities.

This lack of understanding, combined with a growing societal trend to neglect our children's emotional development, may lead to a generation of children Dr. Kyle Pruett of Yale University's Child Study Center calls alarming. "We're potentially raising overly-aggressive children who react to situations with intimidation and bullying, instead of cooperation and understanding: children who won't be able to tolerate frustration, wait their turn, or respect the needs of others."[4]

What are the implications for early faith formation from these studies? First, faith is being "learned" much earlier than we have previously thought. A four-month-old in the grips of a deep depression is emotionally and spiritually needy. This new knowledge should challenge many of the accepted ways children are raised. If my child can be exposed in the womb to music that soothes, I, for one, will be listening to that kind of music. If a four-month-old can become depressed, then we need to become aware and responsive to these signs by giving such a baby extra care, extra comfort, particularly sensitive handling, and prayers that surround his or her crib with protection. A child can be spiritually needy at an incredibly young age.

SPIRITUALLY INTUITIVE PARENTS
UNDERSTAND A CHILD'S EARLY SPIRITUAL NEEDS

Our guess is that the results of these newest studies are simply confirming what the most intuitive parents among us have sensed all along.

One eighteenth-century hymn writer even hinted at the early sensing of babies in existential crisis:

> As soon as born the infant cries,
> For well his spirit knows,
> A little while, and then he dies,
> A little while, and down he lies,
> To take a stern repose.[5]

My mother's responsiveness to my early signs of spiritual need is how I eventually came to my own faith in God. Once I discovered that my mother's God was comforting and accessible, I was soon ready to take the next step to make Him my own. This was as natural as it was real for me.

At the time, Mother and some of her friends ran a backyard Bible club. I was a tagalong, too young to be a real participant, as the club was geared for elementary-age children. But every week I heard her present the plan of salvation. She spoke of God's love and gift of His Son. She spoke of sin and forgiveness. Mostly it was an inattentive crowd. To bring some order to the chaos, she gave away goldfish to children who brought friends with them, or who had memorized their assigned Bible verses, as well as for other behaviors she wished to reinforce.

One afternoon, during this season of nighttime terror, listening to my mother describe God's love, I knew I wanted to come to Jesus. It was strong, this pull, as overwhelmingly appealing as my fears had been unbearably terrifying. I stepped forward and asked Jesus to "come into my heart."

My mother was thrilled, but a little concerned that I might have been drawn to accept Christ as my Savior in hopes of receiving one of those precious, orange, eye-bulging goldfish. Maybe she wondered herself if I was too young to really get it. So on the way home in our car, as I was standing in the front seat beside her, one arm around her neck, the other grasping a plastic bag with my new precious gold-fish, my mother began her questioning.

"Valerie, do you know what it means to accept Jesus as your Savior?"

"Of course [silly mother]! It means that I am changed and I am not a sinner anymore!"

Well, the theology was a little weak. But my salvation experience was authentic. I was still a sinner, as "Goldie" would prove later that week when she floated to the top of the fishbowl—a victim of White Shoulders "aroma therapy." But I was also still saved and growing in relationship with both my parents and God.

This faith, which began almost whimsically—well, it's a conversion story that stands apart from most—has become the bedrock of my life. All through these years, faith has been my comfort and correction, my guide and source of fulfillment in my life's work. My faith has made me feel connected for a lifetime.

WHAT'S SWEETER (AND MORE POWERFUL) THAN THE FAITH OF A CHILD?

The spirituality of children is a wonder and full of mystery. What's more precious than the faith of a child? As young parents we knew the utter delight of cuddling a child who lisped baby faith to heaven on peanut-butter-kissed prayers and Sunday school lilted choruses. The joy for parents in such moments is so exquisite—as if all of life's pleasures were contained in your heart at once, aching to burst out into sweet little pieces from the wonderful pain of it all.

We can't help but think that if the faith of a child is this delight-ful to a human parent, this baby love must reach the heart of a heavenly Father as well. Does God honor early believing? Yes, in ways we can hardly imagine. There's evidence that there may be more to children's faith than we will ever know on this side of heaven. As King David wrote, "With praises from children and from tiny infants, you have built a fortress. It makes your enemies silent, and all who turn against you are left speechless" (Psalm 8:2 CEV).

From God's perspective, baby faith has a special role in the spiritual cosmos. Those peanut butter prayers and Sunday school choruses—praises from the lips of babies—have an amazing impact on evil with eyes to perceive. Those spiritual forces from the darkest of places who oppose God, those who are against God, those who rule the abyss of darkness are stunned into silence. Baby faith leaves hell speechless!

It's difficult for us to get our earthly minds around the spiritual cosmos. We can hardly grasp the otherworldly aspects of the lives we now live. But we can't help but wonder, when we read about a fortress whose brick and mortar are the prayers of children, if maybe that's why a toddler girl's repeated verses of praise in a dark bedroom almost fifty years ago were able to inexplicably comfort her. Perhaps those words of infant faith drove away—actually stunned into silence and impotence, as it were—the very real evil that wanted her soul for a lifetime.

We can't say for sure, but we have to wonder about that sometimes.

If we've learned anything about spiritual formation in children that we are sure about, it's to honor, not underestimate, baby faith. We think if a child is never too young to be taken seriously by God or to be taken seriously by evil, then we parents should be just as aware and responsive to our children's early spiritual needs. We wonder what's more spiritually powerful than the faith of a child.

Jesus babies are the real thing. The powers of darkness and oppressors of infants, those who would destroy the tiniest human spirit know it. They tremble at baby faith. And if you parent a child—it might just shake you a little as well with awe and wonder that—you also parent an eternal soul.

There is no such thing as too young for God.

N O T E S

1. Wilma Burton, *I Need a Miracle Today, Lord* (Chicago: Moody, 1976), 30.
2. Ronald Kotulak, "When Love's Not Enough . . . Nurturing Neurons," *Chicago Tribune,* 15 October 2000, sec. 2, p. 1.
3. Ibid. This joint study by Zero to Three, Brio Corp., and Civitas, three organizations devoted to the welfare of young children, was published in 2000.
4. Ibid.
5. Christopher Smart, *Hymns for the Amusement of Children,* as quoted in David Lyle Jeffrey, *English Spirituality in the Age of Wesley* (Grand Rapids: Eerdmans, 1987), 337.

One generation makes known
your faithfulness to the next.
. . . .

—ISAIAH 38:19b (TLB)

4

Lesson Four

THE "WASTED" MOMENTS ARE FULL OF FAITH-SHAPING POTENTIAL

S ay this about parenting: staying fully engaged with your kids, or "being there," is a challenge. One of our perpetual struggles over the years has been finding time to be together as a family. We felt like we were always juggling our schedules, running around with our hair on fire, and too often missing each other. We also recognized we had a tendency toward taking a few shortcuts along the way even when we were present in body—we were practiced at a version of "being there," but in reality, could still be missing in action.

After all, sharing a house together doesn't necessarily guarantee anyone's authentically sharing life together.

It wasn't so much our own children who taught us this lesson. We learned this one from an unexpected and unlikely source—a little girl named Molly. She was a neighbor child whose parents were involved in a lot of energy-draining adult activity—working two jobs, divorcing, then remarrying each other, divorcing again, establishing new careers, and finally remarrying other people. Though they loved her, they tended to be "otherwise occupied." Most neighborhoods have families living under these kinds of stresses.

Molly decided to try us—and became an inescapable, omnipresent, I-wanna-be-in-your-family neighbor girl. After a while, we gave up trying to establish the usual appropriate boundaries, finding it much easier just to include her and think of her as family.

Her "Fisher-Price stage of life" was a particular challenge for us. During this period eight-year-old Molly lugged her Fisher-Price tape recorder along on her daily visits. She taped everything at our house with no apologies for this intrusion into our privacy. She taped our conversations and our prayers at dinnertime. She recorded Valerie rehearsing to sing a song at church. Our table conversations, whenever she ate with us, were hers forever. In a sense it was our own neighborhood version of reality broadcasting—ongoing special Bell editions of *The Truman Show.*

We all knew it was funny, even Molly. We teased her and goaded her with outlandish storytelling and obnoxious performances, but we never asked her *why* she was recording us. We just blew it off as charming, eccentric, childish behavior. That is, until we realized her intentions. Think of it. If no one at home had taught you to pray, if no parent had ever told you that you could trust God, if you were eager to learn with an insatiable curiosity about spiritual things but traveling alone in your faith journey, then when you were afraid at night, or when you were worried—when you felt too small, too helpless, or too hopeless—the closest way you could come to God might be to turn on your little tape recorder and listen to your neighbors laughing, praying, singing, or talking about God together. You might even sing along there in your darkened room and be comforted knowing that every time you pushed that little plastic play button, God came a little closer and your childhood became a little less empty or spiritually lonely.

And that is what Molly did. This child, from a thoroughly secular home, was on a "no-parent" spiritual journey—all alone. What she was looking for was someone to travel with her. That's why, she revealed later, she picked us.[1]

She's grown-up now and is a committed Christ follower. More recently she started doing full-time youth ministry—helping other kids who are traveling alone spiritually. We couldn't be more proud of her. She's fabulous! True story—with a great ending to date.

WHEN NO PARENT SHOWS UP

But you only have to read the papers to realize that stories about children often come with too many not-so-happy endings. As a nation we are puzzled. We mourn school violence in the aftermath of shootings at places like Columbine High School in Littleton, Colorado. We wonder collectively how to "fix" our kids. Why are they shaping to anger, despair, and violence?

Leonard Pitts, a *Chicago Tribune* columnist, wrote poignantly recently of our need as parents to begin courageously accepting responsibility for our children in the aftermath of a school shooting at Woodson Middle School. In this case, a turf argument between rival New Orleans middle school gangs led to a shooting that left two middle school boys critically wounded. He wrote:

> People have a tendency to identify symptoms but not diseases when tragedy rips through our collective conscience. We blame Hollywood, the video game industry, the gun makers, the members of the rival gangs. Not that they don't deserve the blame. It's just that if you're searching for deeper answers, you can't stop there. You have to understand that American families are fracturing and many of our children are falling through the gap.
>
> And you have to listen to the story Rosalyn Dabney, a parent advocate at Woodson, told a local reporter. It seems there was to be a meeting at the school for parents. She advertised it by posting flyers throughout both housing projects.
>
> Not one parent showed up, she said. Not one.
>
> Therein lies a question not just for the parents of a poor neighborhood in New Orleans, but for parents in all kinds of neighborhoods all over the country:
>
> How can we expect other people to show concern for our children if we do not?
>
> If we haven't gone to the school, shown up for the game, BEEN INVOLVED, how can we blame others for not caring enough? It's

convenient and self-exonerating to always point to external forces in the moral maiming of our children. But their guilt doesn't prove our innocence.

Consider that, as her son lay in surgery, one of the boys' mothers complained that "somebody at school should have known . . . what was going on." But how can somebody at school be expected to know what somebody at home apparently did not?

Meanwhile, Rosalyn Dabney watched hordes of angry, frightened parents descend on the school, demanding answers. It was, she said, the first time many of them had been there.[2]

How can we respond except to say that a lot of American kids appear to be on a "no-parent" journey?

WHEN A KID TAKES A "NO-PARENT" JOURNEY

All of us are becoming too familiar with these kinds of stories. We are becoming too familiar with school violence. But what does this have to do with shaping faith in a child?

It is very subtle, but examine with us for a moment a certain twist in the "being there" struggle. Although it's true that most Christian parents eagerly provide their children with experiences or services, such as a private Christian education, home schooling, chauffeuring to youth meetings and Sunday school—and without a doubt they are well intended as they fund opportunities for their kids to attend Christian camps or perhaps go on a short-term missions trip—in reality, it's possible that on a daily basis very little spiritual exchange may actually be occurring directly between parent and child. This, too, in a very real sense can be a "no-parent" spiritual journey. It is perhaps the greatest oversight of our present-day generation of Christian parents. But how is this possible? How can this be happening?

A lot of our problems in connecting soul to soul with our children has to do, believe it or not, with our prosperity. Ours is a wealth of pleasures that mostly isolate us from each other: video games, mostly played alone; computers with the fringe absorbing benefit of the Internet; TVs; telephones; separate bedrooms; private baths; kids with their own cars. Such "blessings," steeped as they are in independent entertainment and convenience, can become spiritually debilitating to family togetherness and ultimately to faith formation taking place in children's lives. Entertainment used to bring families together. Now it may be having the opposite impact—isolating us farther from each other.

In 1998 the toymaker Hasbro created Family Game Night in an effort to market soft sales of board games. In focus groups with families, they asked children, "Would you play games with your parents?" The answer, "We'd love to, but we don't think our parents want to." Hasbro asked parents the same question. "Would you play games with your kids?" The answer? "We'd love to, but we don't think they would want to."[3]

As much as we hate the idea of all these families missing out on Yahtzee, Scrabble, Battleship, Monopoly, or Axis and Allies, we realize it's not just the glue of board game playing that's gone from family life these days. Think of how differently families live today than they did in earlier times. Previous generations shared so much more of life together. Meals were together, work was together, homes were smaller, a family approach to business was common. Life, in general, was just more intimate.

CHILDREN AT RISK IN OUR HOME AND YOURS

In what has been called a "fundamental clarion call," the National Academy of Science—the most prestigious scientific body in the United States—has issued a somber report on the well-being of American children.

America is rapidly changing for the worse for an increasing number of children. Modern life seems to be throwing more potentially brain-harming experiences in the way of youngsters at the same time when nurturing relationships are being diminished. Modern life is becoming vastly different than [it was in] the recent past and the impact on families is as great as the shift from an agrarian society to an industrial one at the end of the 19th century.[4]

This report cited the profound change in child rearing in the United States during the past three decades. "Half of all children are now in some form of child-care by six months of age, and one of five children [lives] in poverty, which significantly increases a child's risk of a broad range of behavioral problems, learning disabilities and dropping out of school."

The report pointed out as well the risk to children of all economic classes.

> Given how overwhelmingly important relationships are, and the time that's needed to build these relationships, and the fact that family stress is so widespread, the risk for young children is much more pervasive than just children who are living under poverty. Youngsters who lack at least one loving and consistent caregiver, such as a parent or attentive child-care provider, may suffer from severe and long-lasting developmental problems.[5]

No doubt middle-class prosperity and the American Dream are being realized in more families—even if it means both parents are missing in action in order to provide such material comforts. But the dream can become a nightmare. What's at the greatest risk here? When Dad and Mom aren't present, or when they are and they're not really "there," not fully engaged, then there is no spiritual involvement of parents in their children's souls. For many children, a distant Mom or Dad translates into a distant God—for their lifetimes!

That's the risk many Christian parents unknowingly take.

SHARING LIFE WITH MOM
AND DAD—THERE'S NO SUBSTITUTE

As young parents, Valerie and I had hoped for and counted on a lot of help in exposing our children to spiritual things. We prayed that they'd encounter interested teachers along the way. We did all that we could to ensure they were involved in peer groups that were healthy. We provided them with lots of Christian books and music. We required church and youth group attendance. Our children were blessed to experience all of this. But, as beneficial as those resources were, we learned that, bottom line, when it came to faith formation, nothing could substitute for sharing life with a parent. There is just no replacement.

We couldn't look to the schools or churches or social structures to rear our children. We had to learn how to make our home the spiritual formation center our children so desperately needed.

Whenever we'd ask the question, "What does this child need?" it could never be denied that the most primary answer was *spiritually involved parents!* The task before us was to learn how to parent a child's soul—to "know" each of our children on the spiritual level better than any other person in their lives knew them. Yes, we could try to cut corners on "being there," but it was an enormous gamble with potential high risks at stake.

Who among us hasn't wondered how some parents are totally unaware that their kids are building bombs in the family garage or stocking up an arsenal of arms at home? Most of us want to distance ourselves from such possibilities. But the real question is not, Do parents know what is being built in the garage or stockpiled in the closet? The more important question is, Do parents know what is forming in their children's souls? Are our children shaping to anger, shaping to depression, shaping to isolation? Where exactly are our kids—spiritually?

Joseph Califano, president of the National Center on Addiction and Substance Abuse, recently announced the results of a survey taken on over one thousand teenagers between the ages of twelve and seventeen. The teenagers were polled on their use of drugs, including heroin, cocaine, cigarettes, marijuana, and the drug Ecstasy.

Of the teens surveyed, 47 percent said that with "hands-on" parents —defined as parents who were involved in monitoring their children's TV viewing and Internet use, who knew what music their children listened to, where they spent their free time, and where they were after school and with whom—they would be much less likely to use drugs. But one in five teens said they lived with "hands-off" parents.

Califano reported that parents were the biggest deterrents to drug use in kids. "It is the family that will have the greatest impact on this problem. If we are going to solve this problem, it is going to be solved across the kitchen table."[6]

LEARNING TO GRAB THE "WASTED" MOMENTS

Around the kitchen table, in the car while traveling, walking together at the mall, or during a relaxing homework-free evening when the kids are passing time with their music playing behind closed doors, whenever the opportunities arise, it's essential that parents learn to grab the "wasted" moments to get to know their kids.

We "tripped" upon this important concept of capturing the "wasted" moments en route to other goals. Back in the mid-1980s when our boys were still very young, with the help of a modest inheritance due to the untimely death of both of Valerie's parents, we were able to purchase a small cabin near the Great Smoky Mountains National Park of western North Carolina. We were far from wealthy—hardly your classic second-home owners type. Our decision, understandably, created some eyeball rolling with our nearby friends and extended family members. "Are you kidding? North Carolina? But it's so far away. A twelve-hour trip one way with little boys in the car? What's up with that? What are you thinking? Sounds horrible."

And talk about isolated! There was nothing but mountains and forest and streams and family for as far as the eye could see. This was not Disney World—not even close. What *were* we thinking?

We were thinking fun, wilderness living, and adventure. And we were not disappointed. We got that. We also got much more. Traveling down the interstate highway together for hours on end, we discovered that most illusive element of family life—time together—without the interruptions of phones or schedules or social obligations . . . time *together* was ours. During more than fifteen years (with three or more trips each year) we have enjoyed many great and l-e-n-g-t-h-y talks on about every topic imaginable, did Bell family sing-alongs with music cassettes, played Bible memory games, told stories about when Valerie and I were little kids, laughed with Garrison Keillor and public radio's *The Prairie Home Companion* programs, listened to entire books on tape: have lost ourselves in the stories of *The Lion, The Witch, and The Wardrobe,* and others like *Watership Down* and *The Hobbit.* We've memorized entire Abbott and Costello routines, as well as select passages of Scripture. The boys learned to sing by memory all of the lyrics from musicals like *Les Miserables, Fiddler on the Roof,* and *Annie.* We philosophized, and theologized, told stories, and revealed pieces of personal histories about ourselves as well as about extended family members. Over the years and during the thousands of miles we've trekked together, we've debated, listened to each other, prayed together, dreamed of the future, clarified our family values, and time and again have expressed individually and collectively what we think this Bell family is really all about.

We connected. And this was just during the rides back and forth!

The small cabin also had its own unique way of bringing us together. The layout is simple. Apart from a couple of back bedrooms, there's only a great room with a loft—you can't get away from each other if you tried! Nights were often spent in front of a fireplace reading or trying to cream each other in board games or watching videos together. Maybe someone would look up from a book and share a passage out loud with everyone else, which generated comments and discussion. Dirt bikes, whitewater rafting excursions, walking sticks, and campfires were some of the common props for enjoying nature and each other. We regularly reversed our days and nights—oblivious to the outside world—staying up late and sleeping in. We even ate differently at the cabin—more slowly, mealtimes were events to be relished—as we developed a cherished tradition for the normal things of life we pass over too quickly and that completely go unnoticed at home. I, the father, more so even now, will cook on occasion when we're together in the mountains. Believe me, that's really saying something!

The boys are grown now—ages twenty-six and twenty-two—but we still share life at the cabin in ways our "real" lives prohibit. In fact, Brendan and Justin have said to us repeatedly through the years, "You'll probably sell the house in Wheaton someday, and that's OK. We'll understand. But, please, don't ever sell the place in the mountains!"

Yes, as it turned out we had *more* time together because of the hideaway in the Smokies. But also, along the way, we learned to look very differently at some of those everyday occasions typically thought of as just wasted time. These "wasted" interludes or moments are opportunities full of faith-shaping potential.

A CONFESSION

Before having a family, it's fair to say that Valerie and I expected we'd be pretty good at doing the more conventional family devotions approach with our kids. Before the boys came along we anticipated that most evenings following dinner we'd read Scripture together, review memory verses, faithfully pray for select missionaries overseas, and so on. This was the normal pattern in the home where I was raised. My parents were terrific at maintaining such a routine during my childhood, and for the most part it was valuable time together. Especially the aspects they made fun. For example, the missionaries we'd pray for regularly would always be served a meal at our dinner table whenever they were visiting on furlough. I remember so many of these remarkable kingdom people who were fascinating to get to know, with all of their incredible stories of God at work around the globe. From an early age I had concluded that doing ministry in difficult places was an exciting adventure, something worth giving your life to!

Also, Mom and Dad turned memorizing Scripture verses into a contest or competition among us kids. Being the youngest of three, and more competitive than my older brother and sister, this really worked for me. I was good at it! However, I can't say my motives for "hiding God's Word in my heart" were always the purest. Even so, it's a skill and a discipline that has served me well through the years, thanks to my persistently prodding parents who were wise enough to make it a joyful process.

So what about devotional times with *our children*—or with yours? Those times may not always work as well as you would like. Though they are worth pursuing, there are other approaches to focusing your children on spiritual truths.

As was true in my growing up experience, both Valerie and I envisioned that this more formal approach of a regular family devotional time would work for us. We were convinced early on that this kind of spiritual education at home was the primary tool that shaped a child's faith. That was our ideal. Then we had kids. And quite honestly, in our situation it didn't come together exactly like we had envisioned.

We just have not been very consistent at the more traditional family devotional or educational methodologies, although we do honor parents who are disciplined and excel in this arena. We support such approaches. Kudos to you who can make it work. Our particular household, however, was never able to settle in to an established routine that clicked for us over the long haul. End of confession.

LEARNING SPIRITUAL LESSONS AS YOU SHARE LIFE TOGETHER

But we did develop some "on the foot" life skills of connecting with our kids spiritually. And we learned that our children's receptivity to spiritual life seemed to be directly related to the relationship we were enjoying together. The spiritual lessons we tried to give our children seemed to stick best when they were spotlighted in the midst of sharing life together. If you think of family spiritual time strictly as educational time, or as formal devotional time—the time spent sharing Bible curriculum and praying around the family dinner table—then we'd like to challenge you a bit and expand your thinking to include another way as well. Relationship is a fabulous tool to use when it comes to shaping a kid's faith.

You may not have access to a remote cabin, but there are other ways to get away from the pulls on your family and the spiritually debilitating and isolating pleasures of modern life. Think of other possibilities to come together to share life. Be very intentional now and then, and, of course, be realistic. Select special times designated as "family time"—perhaps a Sunday brunch, or Friday pizza dinner, or whenever you can come together as a family to catch up on what's happening with each other. Designate such times as "reserved." Camping brings lots of families together. Family day trips or occasional weekend getaways—even if it's just visiting out of town friends or grandparents—can also provide this same kind of quality downtime. We know of families who have developed family hobbies or special ministries that have provided needed time to really connect. Or here's another doable one: play board games together. We're serious!

What we're describing is sharing life! It is the best environment for teaching about God. We were amazed to realize how much time—time spent running errands; doing household chores; helping with homework; exercising; traveling to and from rehearsals, music lessons, and practice fields—can be redeemed to be more than simply non-productive downtime. We became very intentional in trying to manage this kind of time better. We started thinking of our children as American Express kids—you know, you can't leave home without them—and would grab one or both of them (and sometimes even one or two of their friends) to come along whenever we ran errands. We would use car time to get into their worlds. We'd listen to their music. We got to know their friends. We learned their likes and dislikes. We grabbed those "wasted" moments to find out who this kid was. We also shared who we were and who we believed God to be. We shared our values, our hopes, our faith.

We would be less than honest if we failed to admit that sometimes our children didn't buy in to our agendas. They were resistant now and then. Other families, the schools, even the church at times, challenged our time and space with our kids. Occasionally we felt like interventionists, insisting on family time in a culture that values it so little. But bottom line, only *we* could slow the pace and edit out the isolating pleasures and pulls of modern life. If our family was going to experience any spiritually connective time at all, Valerie and I had to be relentlessly proactive to take the initiative to capture and redeem the opportunities.

Jesus knew how to redeem the "wasted" moments. As mentioned in an earlier chapter, just a couple of years ago Valerie and I visited Israel for the first time. Once we got our bearings oriented to the geography—seeing biblical landmarks and sites that we had over our lifetime studied and read stories about—it became very clear to us that a lot of the time Jesus spent with His disciples was time spent walking from one place to another. Most of the time, when stories were told and values were clarified, was foot travel time—not necessarily formal teaching time. The "downtime" of a walk from Jerusalem to Galilee with His disciples must have been a highly relational time. Maybe they sang as they walked the dusty roads, or teased each other as only people who know each other well can do. We can only speculate. But we can be quite sure the relationships that were established while Jesus and His followers were traveling together provided the setting for bonding and learning. Shared life with Jesus became shared faith. The relational grid became the spiritual grid.

Valerie and I couldn't help but compare that lifestyle with our own. "Foot time," or downtime, is exactly the kind of time most families lack today. Most family members these days are like ships passing in the night—but at incredibly fast speeds! No wonder we are missing each other and thereby lacking the time to bind our hearts together along the way.

DEUTERONOMY 6
FOR THE TWENTY-FIRST CENTURY

How do we translate to our own time the values of verses like Deuteronomy 6:5–9?

So love the Lord your God with all your heart, soul, and strength. Memorize his laws and tell them to your children over and over again. Talk about them all the time, whether you're at home or walking along the road or going to bed at night, or getting up in the morning. Write down copies and tie them to your wrists and foreheads to help you obey them. Write these laws on the door frames of your homes and on your town gates. (CEV)

Perhaps it would read something like this:

Dads and Moms,

Love the Lord your God with all your heart, soul, and strength. (Some things should never change!) Memorize His laws—personalize and obey them—and never stop telling your children about them. Talk about them all the time—whether you're eating a meal together or grabbing fast food en route to a soccer game, whether you're running errands in the car or working on chores at home. Whether you're skiing or watching sports on TV, shopping or waiting in the dentist's reception room—always look for ways to turn the conversation to spiritual things. Carve out connecting time so that your children will know that wherever you go, whatever you do, God and His ways are integrated into your life, a priority in your home, and honored in your heart.

CONNECTIVE TALK—
THE FOUNDATION FOR SPIRITUAL TALK

Taking the time and opportunity to build relationship with a child is an investment in that child's developing soul. Relationship makes a parent's values stick. That's *all* their values, including their love for God. Time together will give you opportunity for "connective talk." What is that? It's conversation that lets you connect with your kids in order to know them—and let them know you—better. How do you do that? Try sharing with each other any or all of the following:

1. What was (is) your childhood like?
2. What were (are) your happiest memories?
3. What childhood pets did you have?
4. Who are you most like, your father or your mother; and who were they most like?
5. Describe how you came to faith in Christ. Be sure to include complete "before and after" descriptions of your life.
6. What was the worst thing you ever did as a kid—and the worst thing they have ever done as kids (self-reporting)?
7. Who most influenced you growing up? For your young children, ask: What people are you drawn to and why?
8. For both parents and kids: What are your favorite movies, foods, pastimes, books, music, colors?
9. Which Bible character do you most relate to and why?
10. When have you felt most close to God?
11. What do you like best about yourself and each other?
12. What would you change, if you could, about yourself? Then ask: What would you change about each other?
13. What do you think heaven will be like?
14. What are your favorite Bible verses? Quote them and tell why they're your favorites.
15. Mention a time when you were afraid or lonely or really angry.
16. Talk about a problem God recently helped you solve.

17. Explain a current problem you need God to solve (parents go first).
18. Name people whom God used you to help in some way; then describe how it made you feel.
19. Mention some of the best things you like about church.
20. Name your most memorable (for better or worse) Sunday school or classroom teacher.
21. Describe the time you laughed in church when you were not supposed to be laughing.
22. Imagine, then articulate a bright future for your child based on his or her greatest characteristics.
23. Talk about the difference God has made in your lives and your family.
24. Mention an area for improvement for both of your lives (self-reporting).
25. Describe a time when you were moved by the Holy Spirit to do or say or be something unusual.
26. Talk about a time you suspected an angelic helper in your life.
27. Explain in detail a time God answered a prayer for you with fireworks!
28. Mention a time God didn't answer your prayer, and now you are so glad!
29. Describe what the consequences of sin look like in people's lives.
30. Discuss God's track record of faithfulness in your lives.

Any of these topics and questions, and hundreds we haven't mentioned, offer opportunity for "shared life" talk. Our list simply models the kind of relationship talk that fosters spiritual receptivity in children.[7]

WELCOME YOUR CHILDREN, AND YOU'LL SEE WONDERFUL SPIRITUAL THINGS

When children are welcome in our lives, wonderful spiritual things can happen. Learning to share your God with your child while you're sharing life together may be the critical skill that fast-paced living requires from our parenting generation.

Picture yourself, for example, in conversation with your kids right there in aisle 7 of the nearby Home Depot, or riding your bikes to the ice cream store, or shopping for basketball shoes at Foot Locker, or doing whatever, whenever . . . all the while binding each other's hearts toward God and toward one another.

Whatever you do, be sure your kids aren't taking a "no-parent" spiritual journey through life. When we think of the loneliness and isolation experienced by so many children today, we can't help but wonder if what's eating at America's children was described by Henri Nouwen when he wrote, "Neurosis is often the psychic manifestation of a much deeper human darkness: the darkness of not feeling truly welcome in human existence."[8]

Maybe that's the message our affluent but isolated lifestyles have given our kids. Maybe our pace is conveying a message of unwelcome. Maybe that's why they're sad and angry and feeling hopelessly disconnected. Maybe that's why they're toting guns to school and building bombs in the garage. Maybe that's why drugs seem so appealing.

It's critical for Christian parents to take up the "being there" challenge so crucial to their children's spiritual formation. Time builds relationship, and relationship is the door our children walk through to God. It's a very clear pattern. Children like Molly are rare. Most "no-parent" journeys in life do not lead to God. Children need parents who know how to travel toward God together.

We applaud the families all around us who are making the nearly heroic efforts to care and connect, to "be there" for their kids. We know this is a very strong cultural current to swim against—practically an undertow in today's culture. And so we are always encouraged to witness this kind of connecting in other families.

Like this snapshot moment from a young pastor's family. Steve and I had been the guest speakers at a churchwide family camp. At the end of the weekend, members of the congregation requested that their young pastor and his wife give a demonstration of the ballroom dancing lessons they had been taking. We were a captured audience as we watched this beautiful couple waltz together around the straw floor of the barn. But best of all, while they turned and gazed into each other's faces, while they stepped and turned, the entire time, their two-year-old was hanging on Daddy's back.

That's sharing life. That's grabbing the "wasted" moments. That's a picture of Deuteronomy 6 for the twenty-first century—whether you're walking or dancing, golfing or eating together—the relationship you build in those times is the best framework in which to teach your child the things you know about God. Share this dance of life with your children. The ordinary daily exchanges of life—in the car to almost anywhere, playing ball, having a tea party with a little girl and her dolls, sitting together doing anything or nothing at all—any of these (and more) are potentially holy moments, opportunities to express, "Welcome to my life. Share my journey with me. Share my God as well. We will do this journey together."

NOTES

1. You can read more about Molly's story and accept the challenge to respond to similar ministry opportunities where you live in Valerie's book, *Reaching Out to Lonely Kids* (Grand Rapids: Zondervan, 1994). For information on ordering this resource, see page 191 at the end of this book.
2. Leonard Pitts *Chicago Tribune,* "In Violence Between Kids, We Refuse to See It's Our Fault," 3 October 2000, sec. 1, p. 13.
3. Leonard Pitts, *Chicago Tribune,* "The Family That Plays Together . . . ," 12 December 2000, sec. 1, p. 29.
4. Ronald Kotulak, *Chicago Tribune,* "Report Says U.S. Fails Kids at Crucial Time," 4 October 2000, sec. 1, p. 4.
5. Ibid.
6. Terry L. Dean, *Chicago Tribune,* "Parents Called the Key to Kids Avoiding Drugs," 22 February 2001, sec. 1, p. 6.
7. For another useful way to develop conversation that connects, see Resource Article 3, "'Getting to Know You': A Family Game."
8. Henri Nouwen, *Life of the Beloved: Spiritual Living in a Secular World* (New York: Crossroad, 1996), 28.

For he orders his angels to protect you wherever you go. They will steady you with their hands to keep you from stumbling against the rocks on the trail.

· · · · · · ·

—PSALM 91:11–12 (TLB)

5

Lesson Five

THE HALLS
ARE FULL
OF ANGELS

What do we make of children's faith? It can be so open and winsome, yet quirky; at times it can be mystical, though perhaps theologically shaky; but most of all—it's so not adult-like! No wonder parents find children's faith both fascinating and puzzling.

We remember a young mother who described to us her conflicted feelings over a conversation she'd had with her first-grade son. Like many parents, in the aftermath of the Columbine shootings, she had serious doubts about the safety of public schooling for her child. Before that incident this mother, whom we'll call Shannon, had held strong convictions about the importance of Christian families staying involved in public school systems, but now she worried about the potential cost of such a commitment. Was Zane safe? Should she enroll him in a private school? Maybe she should seriously consider home schooling him. The maternal urge to protect had shifted into anxious overdrive.

Additionally, Shannon was stymied about how to talk to her son about school safety, concerned that she might alarm Zane by pro-jecting her own anxieties onto him. So one day, as casually as possi-ble, she asked, "Honey, do you feel safe at school?"

"Oh, sure, Mom. Don't worry. The angels take care of us," he reassured her offhandedly.

Thinking the angels comment was just a standard Sunday school answer, the stock Christian kid reply—and with Columbine on her mind *(where were the angels in* that *school?)*—Shannon answered him doubtfully, "Well, let's just hope there actually *are* some at your school."

"Don't worry, Mom," Zane responded. "Our school has lots of angels."

"Lots of angels, really?" she asked, somewhat confused.

"The halls are full of angels," he smiled back at her.

"What? Are you telling me you can *see* them?" she asked, hold-ing back an eerie combination of wonder and doubt.

"Oh yeah!"

And then, unprompted, Zane offered up this additional frosting on the informational cake, "And Mom, don't worry about me at re-cess either. When we go out to play, the angels go in front of us, and the bad angels all run away from our playground."

As Shannon told the two of us this story, we could see that em-barrassment and puzzlement mingled with hope in her heart. "What do you think about it? Could he be telling me the truth? Is he actu-ally seeing angels, or maybe because he's so young, isn't it more like-ly that he's just confused about what he's seeing?"

"Who's confused?" we smiled back as spiritual tingles ran up and down each of our spines. "Your son seems perfectly clear about his school. Only you seem confused!"

She laughed, nodding and still uncertain what to believe.

But let's look at Zane's story. There could be several explanations. Maybe he saw something and confused it with angels, or perhaps he was so worried about his mother that he made all of it up to com-fort her. Those are possibilities. But, then, why rule out the obvious? Is it out of the realm of possibility that God allowed a six-year-old to see angels? And furthermore, have you considered that the specific reason for this "supernatural sightedness" may be for a mother to receive comfort about the rightness of her decision to be "salt" and "light" in an increasingly dark world. Maybe it was a special comfort allowed by God.

TOO GOOD TO BE TRUE?

Bump into the supernatural, and most adults are immediately conflicted. For the adult mind, some things seem just too good to be true.

But Valerie and I have noticed through the years that God frequently operates on a "too good to be true" basis with those He loves—especially with children. Why? Who can say for sure, but we will hazard a couple of guesses. Maybe it's because children are so open to God that it delights Him to honor their special kind of believing with spiritual fireworks from time to time. It's almost as if children are like blank screens on whom God can project Himself. And kids are quick to understand—they "get" Him! Most well-churched adults who are firmly committed to theological accuracy will of course *say* that "with God, nothing is impossible," but children are more apt to actually *believe* it. And because they are unhesitant to believe, they are more readily able to experience such wonders.

So perhaps God reveals Himself supernaturally to children because, in some way, He is just more welcome in their world of possibilities. God rarely breaks in where He is fundamentally unwanted. Children tend to be more open to God with a refreshing capacity to experience Him like adults can't—or won't.

That's one possibility for this special supernatural dimension so characteristic of children's faith—the openness factor. But consider the possibility of another spiritual principle at work here. We've also observed that children who bump into the supernatural early in life, because of such experiences, often have a seal on their heart toward God that stays with them forever. What to many adults may seem like a questionable interpretation of some extraordinary occurrence in a child's life, can actually be a faith-shaping, life-forming experience to a child—one with incredible sticking power.

GOD SETS A SEAL ON YOUNG HEARTS

Consider with us the story of Eli and Samuel from the Old Testament as recorded in 1 Samuel 3. Samuel, Eli the priest's young temple helper, heard a voice in the night calling his name. The young boy thought it was Eli's voice. But when Samuel asked, Eli repeatedly insisted he had not called for Samuel, nor had he heard the voice himself. Only the child could hear the voice in the night. Fortunately, Eli finally realized it was God's voice speaking to the boy, so he urged Samuel to open himself to the Lord, invite Him to speak, then listen up.

Samuel promptly obeyed. And the Lord spoke to him. As a result of this extraordinary call in the night, the Lord was with Samuel as he grew up, and he maintained a remarkable openness to hear and follow the voice of God into his adult years. A lifetime seal was set in Samuel's heart toward God when he was only a young child.

Why would God include such a story in Scripture? Could it be to teach us dads and moms that He reveals Himself to our children in ways that we sometimes miss altogether? When it comes to spirituality, adults don't seem to hear, see, sense, or understand things that are spiritual like children can and do.

Talk openly about this with any group of Christian parents, sharing a story like "the halls are full of angels," and our experience has proven it's not long before other stories start to flow. When the environment is safe enough and the audience accepting enough, it seems many parents have encountered similar occurrences with the faith of their children. Through the years we've heard many parents' stories about their children's "supernatural" experiences. We have found their accounts fascinating. But we've found another dynamic happening at the same time, like a subtheme in most of these unusual stories.

Often, we detect, there is also an element of parental comfort vicariously experienced by the moms and dads of these kids. When life is extreme, it seems God goes to extremes to touch parents with the "supernatural" faith of their children. There's comfort knowing that even when you don't see them, the halls are full of angels.

ANGEL CHOIRS—THE BACKUP SINGERS FOR A WOMAN'S BLUES

A friend told us her story of extreme comfort for extreme pain— all delivered through the faith of her ten-year-old daughter. Lori was grieving the end of her marriage. Her husband had abandoned her and their daughter for Lori's best friend. Double betrayal! Now it was the one-year anniversary of the divorce, and emotional darkness threatened to engulf her. She thought obsessively of her ex and her former friend enjoying themselves together, celebrating their start-over lives as newlyweds.

Her tortured heart could find no relief. Desperate for some deliverance, with tears streaming down her face, she piled her daughter into the car to seek the comfort of her own parents' home five hours away.

"Oh, God," she prayed silently. "You know my heart is breaking, and I don't see any hope or healing in sight. But I will choose to put my trust in you."

Lori remembered the song they had sung in church the previous day and she began to lift her voice in praise to God, even while the tears continued to flow.

> Faithful One so unchanging.
> Ageless One. You're my rock of peace.
> Lord of all, I depend on You.
> I call out to You, again and again.
> I call out to You, again and again.
> You are my rock in times of trouble.
> You lift me up when I fall down,
> All through the storm, Your love is the anchor.
> My hope is in You alone.[1]

After she had sung the chorus several times through, from the back seat of the car her little girl asked, "Mommy, who's singing with you?"

"No one. I'm just singing to myself."

"I hear lots of voices and they're singing with you. Do you have the radio on?"

Lori checked the radio. Maybe it was on low and some sounds were bleeding through. No. It was off. She heard nothing.

Her daughter pressed her case. "They're still singing. They're singing the song you were singing until you stopped. I can hear them."

Lori felt a shock as she considered the too-good-to-be-true possibility of who might be singing with her. Could it be angels? Who else could her daughter be hearing? Comfort beyond human comfort held her close. The obsessive and persistent pain eased as she embraced the sweetness of the moment. "O God, thank You. Thank You for loving me enough to show me I'm not alone, and that I am precious enough, my praise fragrant enough in this pain, that You would accompany it with the sounds of heaven."

GOD'S SUPERNATURAL TOUCH

Too extreme for you to believe? Well, unfortunately, some of the older extended family members who heard this story later brushed it off as childish imaginings right to the young daughter's face. How terribly they mishandled this little girl's faith. She was crushed by the disbelief of the adults. Why choose such a time to nitpick theologically? When it comes to children, how much better to leave the door open for the possibilities that God is sometimes almost "too good to be true."

Marjorie Thompson, director of the Pathway Center for Christian Spirituality, has called upon adults to respect the spiritual sensitivity and learning underway in the hearts of children:

> It is essential in the home as well as in the congregation to understand that children have their own spiritual experiences and perceptions, their own unique inner mystery that belongs to God alone. Children are neither blank screens on which adults may write their scripts nor empty vessels that adults are duty-bound to fill up with doctrine and moral regulations. . . .
>
> Children need their spiritual dimension affirmed and supported; they need firm but loving discipline to give secure parameters to their growth; and they need adults to point faithfully to God with trust and joy.[2]

If you've been spiritually sensitive enough to recognize that God
has come near to a child of yours, then you know how utterly shocking it can be. What is more impacting to life than to realize that God
has actually shown up? C. S. Lewis describes our conflicted feelings
at such moments:

> Men are reluctant to pass over from the notion of an abstract and
> negative deity to the living God. I do not wonder.... It is always shock-
> ing to meet life where we thought we were alone. "Look out!" we cry,
> "it's *alive*."
>
> ...An "impersonal God"—well and good. A subjective God of beau-
> ty, truth and goodness, inside our own heads—better still. A formless life-
> force surging through us, a vast power that we can tap—best of all. But
> God Himself, alive, pulling at the other end of the cord, perhaps ap-
> proaching at an infinite speed, the hunter, king, husband—that is quite
> another matter. There comes a moment when the children who have
> been playing at burglars hush suddenly: was that a *real* footstep in the hall?
> There comes a moment when people who have been dabbling in religion
> ...suddenly draw back. Supposing we really found Him? We never meant
> it to come to that! Worse still, supposing He had found us?
>
> ... There is no manner of security against miracles. One may be
> in for *anything*.[3]

But, what about the whole angel thing? Do rational adults actually believe they exist, or is it just a part of pop culture—a cute idea
that sells mugs and calendars, T-shirts, books, and Christmas orna-
ments? In light of this adult tension, we were very interested to read
Dr. Billy Graham's view on the existence of angels:

> I am convinced that these heavenly beings exist and that they pro-
> vide unseen aid on our behalf. I do not believe in angels because some-
> one has told me about a dramatic visitation from an angel, impressive
> as such rare testimonies may be. I do not believe in angels because UFOs
> are astonishingly angel-like in some of their reported appearances. I
> do not believe in angels because ESP experts are making the realm of
> the spirit world seem more and more plausible. I do not believe in
> angels because of the sudden worldwide emphasis on the reality of

Satan and demons. I do not believe in angels because I have ever seen one—because I haven't.

I believe in angels because the Bible says there are angels; and I believe the Bible to be the true Word of God. I also believe in angels because I have sensed their presence in my life on special occasions.[4]

We have every reason to believe that our lives, our children's lives, our friends' lives, and the lives of those who read this book can bump into the supernatural in the most amazing ways. Scripture itself is flooded with such supernatural accounts. And however wondrous, they were almost always disturbing, sometimes humiliating to the human person who experienced them. Moses' encounter with the burning bush completely redirected the course of his life. Jacob struggled in a supernatural wrestling match that changed his whole identity. Jonah became fish food before he became a prophet. Noah's life was literally a zoo! Mary willingly endured the public shame of an out-of-wedlock pregnancy to give birth to the Savior of the world. But what these people would have missed if they had dismissed these experiences as meaningless! When we are not open to such activity we rule out the creative involvement of God in our lives.

A TIME TO SEIZE THE DAY

So when a little boy reports that the halls are full of angels, when a daughter hears a sing-along choir where there is none, when young ears hear a voice calling his name, what's a parent to do?

These are times to seize the day—for your child and for yourself! Valerie and I learned to stay open to our children's faith at such times—to "seize the day" as one full of spiritual possibilities.

Whenever there's some extraordinary occurrence or an unexplainable spiritual phenomenon in your child's life, the most important concern at such times is *not* to dissect the experience to determine if what took place was legitimately supernatural—who is wise enough to decide that, anyway? What matters most in these moments is whether the emerging faith of the child is being affirmed and encouraged.

Picture these children like new young sproutings. Against many obstacles—their faith is pushing through the soil of life—it's green and alive and stubbornly resistant to the enemies of spiritual growth. Despite hostile climate and predatory spirits and sometimes poor growing conditions—faith is emerging. At this stage, it is too early to tell what this plant will become—iris or corn, oak or ivy, Presbyterian or charismatic, Baptist or Methodist—the doctrinal specifics will come later, but now is the time to celebrate growth. It is definitely not the time to worry if this fits into the right theological tenet. How tragic and far too common it is for a child's tender faith to be cut off at the roots by some well-meaning adult whose own faith has been limited and dulled down by years of resistance or callousness.

Aha! Zane says his school is full of angels. Faith, that most transforming quality of life, is taking root in this child. How fabulous. Put aside any theological hesitations for the moment and celebrate. Your child has eyes that see—nurture his faith. Your child has an open heart to God—tell your friends. This child's life has taken a most wonderful course. Applaud. Encourage. Be amazed. Even if you—rational adult that you are—struggle to believe it yourself.

And if that were not wonderful enough—there is more. These experiences are not just about what is happening to the children. There's more than a child's emerging faith in this mix. It's important for adults to understand that the point of occasional spiritual fireworks in our children's lives is not only to encourage our children's believing but also, very often, to strengthen our own faith. Because we are so joined at the faith hip with our children, God speaks through them in an "attention grabbing" way that gets to us as nothing else can. The outsized faith of a child is one of the more interesting ways God challenges the shrunken faith of a parent.

This double-edged sword of parent-child faith formation is both shocking and delightful to experience. Sometimes, we've noticed, God can even be quite humorous in His "I-am-with-you-and-very-much-alive" methods.

ANGELS GO WHERE DADS AND MOMS FEAR TO TREAD

Valerie first learned this lesson through an unexpected answer to prayer when our first son, Brendan, was in third grade. He was highly motivated to please and eager to be a cooperative member of elementary school life. Every parent-teacher conference was the same. "Your son is a joy. So well behaved, a great follower of directions, never a problem in the classroom." That's why Valerie was unprepared for the events that followed.

On this particular afternoon (Steve was working out of town for a few days) Brendan came home in tears with a different story to tell. He had spent the afternoon in the principal's office. In one afternoon this kid had gone from being an "angel" in the classroom to apparently needing the most severe discipline the school had to offer—the dreaded office of Mrs. Adams!

Through tears he poured out his frustrating story. There had been a substitute teacher for gym that day—a stranger who, apparently, did not know Brendan's in-house reputation for "sainthood." She had been struggling to control the class and at one point looked over and saw three boys fighting. In a desperate bid at establishing her authority, she pointed at the three boys and sent them all packing to the principal's office. Brendan was one of those boys.

"Mom, I tried to tell them we weren't fighting. But no one would listen to me. The two bigger boys were pushing me back and forth like I was a ball between them, but no one was angry, and what was I supposed to do—I'm a head shorter than both of them?"

My reaction? Of course, I believed him. I am his mother. It's part of the job description.

"Don't worry, Brendan," I reassured him. "Mommy will just call Mrs. Adams and get this whole misunderstanding straightened out. I'm sure it's something we can easily clear up." But I was inexperienced in dealing with Mrs. Adams. I had no idea what more seasoned and school-toughened parents went through when negotiating with school authorities.

Expecting a reasonable hearing, I explained my son's dilemma. It was stone silent on the other end. Finally, in slowly measured words—as if she were speaking to someone who was exceedingly dense—the principal said, "When-boys-fight, I-give-them-a-punishment-they-will-not-forget-and-then-we-do-not-see-them-in-here-again." The inflection in her voice placed an enormous period on the end of that sentence. It declared, "The end! We will discuss this no more."

What can I say? I was a desperately protective young mother, wondering what terrible punishment qualified as something Brendan "will-not-forget." I couldn't contain myself. I completely lost my cool. I told her I had been a schoolteacher and that I didn't believe her methods worked as she stated. I knew how things at school really worked. I knew she saw the same children all the time. Furthermore, I informed her that, in my rather qualified opinion, there were more important lessons children needed to learn from adults than just to keep their hands off of each other—children needed to know that adults, to whom their care was entrusted, could be counted on to listen and be fair, for instance.

"Mrs. Bell," she iced into the phone, "you do not teach at this school. I am in charge here and I will see your son in my office every day for the rest of the week." And with that, the conversation was over. Period.

As I hung up the phone I was immediately aware of three things: First, I was decidedly sick to my stomach. Second, I had made a bad situation much worse. And third, I was beginning to learn a big life lesson —and I was learning it right there in the third grade, thanks to Mrs. Adams: In life, there are some things that even "Mommies" cannot fix.

With Steve traveling and far away from home that night, I was flying this "trip" solo. I spent the rest of the evening before bed alone with our son, trying to strengthen him spiritually. "Brendan, I couldn't get her to listen to me either. But let's remember that even Jesus was falsely accused. It happens to the best of us. So, don't be ashamed or embarrassed in the principal's office this week. Let's pray that God will somehow intervene and this will not be such a bad experience in the end."

But in my heart, what I really believed was that there are some things that even God can't fix. What could prayer really do?

Brendan left for school the next morning weighted down with dread. His body slunk onto the school bus—he was sadness personified. I cried over having to send him to a hostile place where I couldn't protect him. Most of the day I barely functioned from the burden of worrying about him.

And so when the school day was over I sadly anticipated the return of my little boy. I knew he would get off that bus just beaten down by life. Finally the yellow school bus pulled up, stopped, opened its winged door, and deposited our son. I recognized his jacket, his backpack, but could this be Brendan? *This* child was laughing and hoppity, skippity, running with joy. He swooshed into the house with a smile that lit my heart like the Rockefeller Center Christmas tree.

"Brendan, what happened today? Did you have to spend the day in Mrs. Adams's office?"

"Oh yeah, Mom, I did. It was great!"

"*Really?* Mrs. Adams's office was great?"

"You'll never guess what happened. You know that cute little girl I really, really like from the fourth grade?"

"Alyssa?" I asked, wondering where this could possibly be going.

"Right. Well, guess who came into Mrs. Adams's office when I was sitting there?" spoken with a big gushy smile. "That's right. Alyssa! And guess who *talked* to me?"

"Alyssa?" I hazarded an obvious answer.

"Uh-huh." (A grunt packed with caveman testosterone and al-pha-male swagger.)

Well, the "before and after" of this child was so dramatically dif-ferent I thought this must have been *some* conversation. "Well, what did this amazing chickie Alyssa say to you?"

"She asked me my name. Mom, she wanted to know who I was! Isn't that great?"

"Yes, that's great. So what did you tell her?"

"Oh, I was too shy to even talk to her. I opened my mouth to talk but nothing would come out, so I just smiled at her. My friend had to tell her my name. We all thought it was really funny."

"You mean you didn't say anything to her?" I asked in wonder-ment, but I'm thinking, *Is there more? Am I missing something here? How could so little change so much?*

"Oh no. I was too shy. Then she asked what we did to get in trou-ble. And I still couldn't talk to her. I just kept smiling, so my friend told her what we did. And she laughed and said, 'You two are really cute.' Mom, she knows who I am! She thinks I'm cute. What a great day. If I hadn't been in Mrs. Adams's office, Alyssa still wouldn't know I'm alive!"

And while I was still pondering *that* "miracle," he threw this in as an aside, "Oh yeah, and Mrs. Adams says she thinks I've learned my lesson, and I don't have to come back to her office again this week."

I laughed so hard the tears, which only the night before had sorrowed their way down my face, now skipped and somersaulted down the same path in joy. Is God creative or what?

Some might say it was only an unusual circumstance or just a coincidence that came into play in our third-grader's life that day—the cosmos didn't shake, the world kept revolving—what's the big deal? But in the Bell home (as we've learned in the ensuing years to practice this same mind-set concerning other situations)[5] we chose to believe that God personally intervened in a delightful, joyful, move-the-mountains kind of way. That day He deployed a ministering child named Alyssa to mend our son's broken heart. And to add frosting to the cake, He accomplished the nearly impossible turnaround of melting the principal's heart toward Brendan as well. Supernaturally, a day of anxiety became one of surprising laughter and joy.

Brendan and I learned a powerful spiritual lesson through that extraordinary experience. On that particular day, a lifetime seal was set in both of our hearts. We had encountered the double-edged sword of God's showing up in our lives. One learning edge was for a child. The other was for the mother. My faith was strengthened to believe that a heavenly Father *can* parent our children better than we can ourselves. It is a faith lesson I have leaned on since. Even now, as both our sons grow into their young adult years—years that mommies (or daddies) often can't fix—I find comfort from that day Brendan (and I) spent in the third grade!

And now that Brendan's in his mid-twenties? Well, he knows that sometimes the halls are full of angels. He isn't one of those adults who struggles to believe that on occasion a guest host of angels just might show up where needed to provide a private audience performance. After all, when you bump into your own personalized "miracle" in the principal's office, you might grow up to be an adult who just never quite gets over it.

GOD *IS* PRESENT

Fine for you, you may be thinking, *but what about Columbine? What about the children in the concentration camps of Auschwitz? Did the angels run scared? When a child dies in a car accident or from disease in a cancer ward, where are the angels then? What do we make of God's care and pro-tection at some points while at others it seems to be absent? When evil and heartbreak win the day are the angels still there?*

Yes—especially then.

The halls are full of angels even when we don't see them, *especially* when we don't see them. Beyond our ability to sense or feel or touch or see, the supernatural world of God exists. Scripture's unmistak-ably clear about this. Even when evil wins a heartbreaking battle, when the cost of darkness is the life of a child, God is present.

At certain times most of us readily believe that God's hand is at work when we're given a glimpse, or a taste, of His presence—some special evidence of divine intervention on our behalf. Any of us can be quick to affirm God's attention to even the smallest of details in our lives. It's not that much of a leap, then, to believe that in more extreme times God is *still* there. His phenomenal creative ability to provide comfort, lead to the light, or minister in remarkable fash-ions seems to us intensified at such times. Who can say what the an-gels might do in the face of terrible predicaments or desperate pain? We can only suggest that they do everything within their supernat-ural power, whatever is allowed by the will of God, perhaps some-thing unheard, unseen, unfelt, or totally unsensed by anyone other than that child in that moment.

God's creative forces are strongest in the darkest places. If He notices enough to minister to a little boy in the principal's office, the possibilities are limitless for what He might do for children in more dire situations.

That's why we've learned to value the belief that the halls *are* full of angels, the principal's office *can* be a place of grace, and the angels can sing backup whenever or wherever they choose. They can do those things even when *we* don't see them, hear them, or sense them in any other way—especially then, for they are there with us and with our dear children all the time.

As a parent, remember to stay open to your children's spirituality and perceptions. Do so, and you may experience a delightful twist of the "normal" order—the very children you seek to spiritually form may comfort and surprise you. It is the open heart that is most likely to receive the comfort God is willing and able to give.

NOTES

1. "Faithful One," Brian Doerksen, © 1989 Mercy ASCAP. Vineyard Publishing. All rights reserved. Used by permission.
2. Marjorie J. Thompson, *Family: The Forming Circle* (Nashville: The Upper Room, 1996), 114–15.
3. C. S. Lewis, *Miracles,* (New York: Macmillan, 1947), 96–97.
4. Billy Graham, *Angels: God's Secret Agents* (Waco: Word, 1975), 14–15.
5. We've practiced "The God Hunt," a family spiritual tool as described in Resource Article 1 (see page 161).

So take a new grip with your tired hands, stand firm on your shaky legs, and mark out a straight, smooth path for your feet so that those who follow you, though weak and lame, will not fall and hurt themselves, but become strong.

· · · · · · ·

—HEBREWS 12:12–13 (TLB)

Lesson Six

RELAX— GOD IS IN THE MESSES

S ome of us just don't get around!" That's how Valerie explains that, for the past nineteen years, the Bell family—Steve, Valerie, Brendan, and Justin—have all lived in Valerie's childhood home. Of course, for Valerie it has lots of good childhood memories . . . and lots of lessons. One of the most important lessons came the year she and the rest of the Burton family moved into the plain-looking foursquare—a typical, white farm-style home, the kind visible from most any country highway you might travel.

Back then, when her parents were looking for a different home, it was eight-year-old Valerie who insisted that this house, where we still live today, was the one they should buy. Here's how those events unfolded so many years ago.

AN EIGHT-YEAR-OLD'S STORY

Though I was very young, somehow I just knew that this good-boned house should become our home. Its stucco constancy would become an ironic subplot in my life. At some level we seem peculiarly bonded—neither able to escape the other. So I have spent most of my life as a child and now as an adult woman here. Why my parents let me have the deciding vote in such an important matter, I have no idea. I only know that of all my family members, I have lived in this home the longest and with the most attachment, so perhaps it was right that my parents allowed me to choose it.

There is so much personal history attached to this place. During my first summer and fall in this home, just before I entered third grade, I learned a particularly important spiritual lesson—one Steve and I continue to marvel at as adults and parents. We believe it has such a fundamental grounding for the soul that through the years we've tried to impress it on our own children at every opportunity. The lesson? Look beyond life's messes. Messes are more than disappointments and heartbreaks. Messes are the directional markers on the soul maps of our lives. Experience a mess and learn to suspect that behind the human confusion or puzzlement or disaster, there will be the activity of God at work in some way. Messes are more than messes—because *God is in the messes.*

That was one of my first spiritual lessons, and I continue to learn the implications of this truth that I began to understand as a third-grader. My no-mess life up to that point had been lived in a quiet, old neighborhood (the neighborhood before the house where we currently live). That neighborhood was one of aging homes and their equally antiquated owners. Our house was just as old—a source of worry to my father, who lost sleep at night envisioning floors giving way beneath us or roof timbers caving in over us.

"EAT OUR DUST, WITCHY WOMAN"

I did not give an ounce of worry over floorboards or ceilings, but judged the quality of our lives totally by our neighbors. I gave it barely a passing grade. No one was mean on our block, but it wasn't exactly a kid-friendly neighborhood either. My younger brother and I were the only youngsters around, and our older neighbors mostly ignored us—except for one—and it was clear to us that this neighbor really hated kids.

She lived on the corner in a huge, stone home, a home with a foreboding, gray medieval exterior that any storybook-literate kid would instantly recognize as a witch's dwelling. The house was scary enough by itself, but the owner looked every bit the part of the occupant of a witch house. Her nose was long, her hair cut straight and severe just below the earlobes. We just knew she had a cauldron brewing in some dank, dark place inside and bats in her belfry!

My younger brother and I were novice bicyclists that summer. But we were confined to sidewalk travel. Bummer. Worse still, our overly protective mother had only one "mother approved" route—the sidewalk around our own block. Crossing the street was strictly forbidden! This was a big problem. It meant we had to go by the witch's house. And worse yet, the sidewalk in front of her corner house was a huge challenge. It was too sharp for beginning bicyclists. The slow speed required to turn the corner produced too much wobble. The *only* solution to this problem was to round off the corner (on the lawn side of her bushes) and cut through the yard.

No big deal to us. But the results were predictable. Inevitably, within seconds of our tire tracks leaving their indents on her precious grass, she would be wildly gesturing on her porch and yelling at our backsides, "Keep off the grass!"

Our first few days of encounters left us wide-eyed and frightened. But as we got speedier we also got brattier. Soon we were full of inappropriate audacity and she'll-never-catch-us bravado. One of the great passages of childhood independence, after all, is realizing that no foot-powered adult can catch you when you're on a bike. Loser! Soon she was always behind us, always history, always eating our dust.

Our daily bicycle rides became dangerous adventures in survival against this evil witch. Even when we learned to make the corner—without wobble—we chose not to. We were addicted to the adrenaline rush that corner provided our bike treks. This had become an exhilarating and treacherous game to us—one with multiple strategies. Sometimes we simply ignored her—acted like we hadn't heard her at all. At other times we evaded her watchful eye and gleefully imprinted the crime scene with tire tracks—a kind of arrogant graffiti we knew she would discover later. Occasionally (if there was enough distance between her and us) we yelled back at her, "You witch! We aren't hurting your stupid grass. Leave us alone."

She never caught us. Better yet, she never complained about us to our parents. Our bald-faced naughtiness was totally and delightfully without any consequences.

CONSEQUENCES: THERE IS A GOD!

That summer we moved across town, into the home of my choice. This much larger home was quite old but very solid—good-boned— and a great comfort to my father, as it was structurally sound both above and beneath. We children gave it better grades as well. The new neighborhood had kids. Our social life was improved. Mother even let us join with the other kids on the block in riding our bikes on the new-to-us, less-trafficked street. Life had taken a decided turn for the better.

Summer vacation finally came to an end, and that September I walked into my third-grade classroom on the first day of school, dressed in new clothes, full of confidence for this new beginning. But new clothes could not lessen the sting of what I would experience that day. I took one look at my new teacher and my unbelieving eyes could barely take her in.

Is this possible? . . . Is she who I think she is? . . . Am I seeing things? . . . Is this just a bad dream? . . . Can it really be true?

Sure enough, it was true. My new teacher—she was the old "witch."

I was shocked. Her beady eyes appraised me from behind dark horn-rimmed glasses that perched over her hooked nose and recognized me instantly as the neighborhood brat. She didn't say anything. She simply smiled a smile that clearly communicated to me, "Gotcha!"

In the time it takes to inhale a breath, my no-mess world came to a screeching halt. Now I would learn how it felt to have the world spinning out of control around me. I felt the emotional quicksand sucking me down and under. I completely panicked. I wanted to run away from that classroom as fast as possible.

But where could I hide? Compounding my problem was that the witch was not the only formidable woman in my life. My mother's favorite Bible verses, recited to me frequently, were "Even a child is known by his doing" and "Be sure your sins will find you out." It was to *this* mother I would have to explain my tears over my new teacher. I would have to tell *this* mother about my absolute fright in finding that the witch was my new teacher, and worst of all, I could not explain why my teacher was the witch without telling all. I would have to confess my secret life as a neighborhood hooligan. My sins, as Mother had predicted, had found me out!

When I got home, my mother's first-day-of-school radar instantly detected that something had gone wrong. And when I told her my story, as I suspected, she was not amused nor was she happy with me. She absolutely refused to intervene for me. Instead, the next day I went to third grade with strict instructions to apologize to my teacher for my summer's worth of relentless rude and uncaring behavior. This was one lesson maternal protection would not deliver me from learning.

Great lesson? Yes, but that's not the best part of this saga. Mrs. Syawalka proved to be much more than a witch—someone who didn't blink at instructing children, neighborhood or classroom, in correct behavior. She was also a woman of great imagination and creativity. (What other kind of woman would choose to live in a witch-like house?) Her great passion was writing. She empowered us with admonitions: "Don't write boring things. Tell me you saw a zebra on your way to school and that it talked to you in Swahili. Tell me you know how to fly and describe what it feels like. Write words that make me smell and taste and feel things that are astonishing. Bring tears to my eyes. Make me laugh. Write with your imagination. Please . . . *please* . . . whatever you do, *please don't bore me!*"

To my amazement she seemed to *like* me. My writing assignments were always returned to me with wonderful comments from her. I guess she believed any little girl who could imagine her next-door neighbor was actually a witch could perhaps also delve a little deeper into that imagination to become (who knows?) a writer someday. She encouraged me exceedingly beyond anything I deserved.

The truth is, the "witch" became one of my all-time-best teachers, the first one to recognize my emerging bent for writing, the one whose admonition to "at least make it interesting" would stick with me even to this day.

But that's still not the best part of this story. Something more important than encouragement to write came from that experience. What I learned in third grade has become a bedrock conviction in my life: God is in *all* of our messes—even those of our own making.

GOD'S IN *EVERY* MESS

Now I'm learning how much more courage it takes to believe this as a parent than it was to learn it as a child. As Steve and I have raised our own children in the shadow of my own childhood experiences, that truth has stuck with me—but with many twists and turns, with subplots of doubt, anxiety, and worry being the unwelcome subtitles in a life oriented to faith. Amazingly, even though I believe deeply in God's creative ability to reorder or "unmess" our lives, it seems I have to relearn this truth with every new mess.

I have discovered that each mess, with its own unique level of disruption, turmoil, or chaos—particularly where our children are concerned—has an original unfamiliar twist, a novel never-before-experienced anxiety, a fresh unanticipated wound, a perverse new challenge. Faith never seems to be a completed work in my life. And so I confess to finding it easier to hold to this tenet—that God is in *all* of our messes—about events of the past, once the perplexity or confusion is resolved, than I do to holding this conviction in the midst of some in-the-present upheaval.

I also am amazed at how much more inclined I am to have faith about God's involvement in my own messes than to hold to that line unwaveringly concerning our children's messes. Problems concerning our children have an incredible power to leave me extremely vulnerable as nothing else can. Here I am fragile, overwhelmed by the motherly urge to protect, at times even to the detriment of their own spiritual learning curves. When our children feel pain I want nothing more than to ease it. Let them learn the lesson sometime when I'm not around to feel it too!

Yes, our kids' messes strike at this bedrock belief that God is involved in every tough situation. Yet when something in our children's lives has us on our knees, when you and I as parents can't "fix" the problem—and we are reluctantly but completely dependent on God's help and intervention—only then do we recognize the double-edged sword of parent-child faith at work in our lives.

WHAT WE PARENTS MUST LEARN TO DO

In the middle of a mess, when an aspect of life seems in disarray, when well-ordered plans or dreams are disrupted, it's not just about the kids anymore. For most of us, God can really grab our attention during such times. It's then that we must give to our children the lessons learned by soul—not just by head. If we want our children to believe that they can trust God, especially in the confusing, uncertain, messy times of life, then we ourselves must hold unwaveringly to this conviction with a bedrock confidence.

How hard is it to have unshakable faith? Sometimes Valerie and I think it is the hardest trick in the whole bag. Families' no-mess lives can come to an end in a second—the second it takes to inhale a shocked breath. In the next breath, it seems, some Christian moms or dads can immediately wonder if God even cares, or if He is involved at all. Parents aren't immune to their own faith crises.

In such times, whenever Valerie or I are tempted to waver, we think about what happens to most children whose parents become shakable at this point of trust. Children whose parents waver at the faith-bends in life can become vulnerable, reacting to their parents' heartaches with a confused bitterness. Now, not only are they facing the crunch of the original problem, but they have also lost the protection of a parent's faith.

Anne Graham Lotz quotes her mother, Ruth Graham, as saying, "You can't teach your children to eat spinach if you won't touch the stuff yourself." If you want your children to have enduring faith—you yourself must grip it tightly when outcomes are uncertain and your own life's securities are slipping away.

"REMEMBERING" STRENGTHENS FAITH

What are we saying? Are we suggesting that parents practice some kind of spiritual hypocrisy, that they wear a mask of trust at all times?

Absolutely not. That would be horrible for both parent and child. Besides, it's impossible to fake authentic spiritual life.

What we *are* suggesting is that the muscle of faith be built up through the years. Trust is a learned habit that becomes stronger with use. We wish we had learned earlier, as younger parents, that every crisis is an opportunity to learn to trust God more, a chance to perceive how He was working in our hearts, another new lesson in how faith is built.

Over the years we have learned to build each other up with a kind of remembering. As a family, when one of us is in a crisis, we will often review our histories of God's ongoing goodness to us in past messes. This remembering is a track record of God's faithfulness in our lives that renews faith in a present struggle. With these "rememberings" we preserve each other's moments of grace, we recall merciful deliverances, and we reexperience joys that transcend time.

Remembering can strengthen a family's faith. It often gets the wobbliness out.

For instance, Justin, our younger son, was going through a period of uncertainty as he was about to graduate from college. That is a very stressful time for most young adults, when there is no determined path. Justin wondered what the next step should be. He considered how life would (or wouldn't) come together. As he walked toward one possibility, he realized that choice might also mean closing other doors.

And then there was that often asked unanswerable question by so many well-meaning folks, "So what are you going to do when you graduate?" During that time, we were talking about this issue with Justin while eating with another family. The conversation became frustrating, and soon we were trying to minister comfort to him with "rememberings."

"Justin, remember how God has worked in the past, especially at those times when everything seemed to be falling apart?

"Remember your freshman year of high school when you didn't make the basketball team because your coach was convinced someone who was a musician couldn't be an athlete too? He actually said that to you. Remember how badly Mom and I felt for you? As your father, I was crushed. I almost took it personally. All of us agreed that what happened to you was completely unfair. It wasn't a question of having the ability—you were a fierce competitor, had the talent, the speed, the shot, the heart. In our collective family wisdom, we were certain that coach had been irresponsibly biased and prejudiced against you. It was terrible!

"But then, in high school, because you only played football in the fall, and ran track in the spring, in the winter you were able to get involved in the school's plays and musicals.

"And watching you on the stage gave us all so much joy—seeing that side of you emerge and develop—it was the best! But you might not have had that opportunity had you made the basketball team. There just wouldn't have been enough time. Looking back it's now obvious: God was in that mess from the get-go.

"And then look at the growth in your life in college. As a freshman you went to the state university as a jock and a performer. But now look at you. You're graduating from college as a very analytical thinker and fabulous writer. Those are incredible learning curves and terrific life skills that God can really use. Those transitions of closed doors and then others opening to you were painful sometimes, we know. But God was in all the college messes too.

"So, Justin, do you possibly think that God won't lead and direct you now? Will He suddenly abandon you after having led you so specifically thus far? You have a great future! And it's going to be a wonderful adventure to discover what God wants to do with your life."

Justin listened in agreement, if not with outright enthusiasm. After all, this is *his* "mess" and it's hard for even the most experienced among us to have an unshakable confidence in the middle of personal complexities and uncertainty.

But something else was happening during that table conversation that day. As we were talking to our son, our friends were listening and the woman began to tear up a little. Her reaction to hearing this spiritual life principle surprised us.

"Hearing you talk is causing me to reflect and reinterpret some events in my own life. I've never put the pieces together until now. I'm fifty-something and have never understood why God closed the doors of cheerleading to me in high school. Cheerleading was such a big deal in my school, and I never made the squad. Every year it was the same routine: I tried out; was rejected; and then, was broken-hearted.

"I can still feel sad whenever I think about it as an adult woman. But just now I'm realizing that not being a cheerleader allowed me time to develop as a pianist and organist. From an adult perspective, that turned out to be an incredibly good trade-off. I can hardly believe it's taken all these years before I got the bigger picture."

BECOME AN EXPERT AT THE BACKWARD GLANCE

Exactly. None of us can grasp the whole picture of our lives without a backward glance that brings God and our experiences into spiritual focus. If we learn sooner than later (hopefully before the age of fifty) that we can trust God to work on our behalf in all of life's messes, then surely we are better off. Like the children of Israel who, when they passed over into the Promised Land, were instructed by God to build "stones of remembrance" to commemorate God's goodness in their past, families too need a way to remember God's faithfulness. It is "remembering" that strengthens faith to face unsure tomorrows.

Become an expert at the backward glance, and your children's faith will be strengthened. Children need to hear their parents' stories. They need the protection of our faith. Do they know what God has done for you in the past? Are they learning the ways that God leads by hearing about the ways God has led you? Have you detected patterns in the way He speaks to you?

More important, have you shared that with your children? What disappointments turned out to be blessings? What heartbreak was softened by some comfort provided by God? How has God strengthened you and ministered to you over the years?

These are your "stones of remembrance," the track record of who God is and how He's communicated His love to you and your family. These are lively conversations for around the dinner table, or when traveling in the family car, or while roasting marshmallows behind the house, or around a campfire during vacation. Or they are delightful topics of discussion to be overheard when company comes. In families where faith is built and strengthened and formed, these "rememberings" are often the recurring themes, the patterns of conversation

—what we can keep returning to so that we can help form faith in one another's souls.

KIDS WANT TO HEAR YOUR STORIES

Children love to hear stories from their parents' pasts, particularly if they reveal some fallen nature in a parent's childhood. "Mom, tell us more about the witch who was your teacher. Was she really a witch? What was it you and your brother did to her?"

"Dad, tell us again about how you spent your entire coin collection going on rides at the county fair. Did you *really* do that? How much did you say those complete sets would be worth today? You used it all up in one afternoon? Did your parents punish you?"

"How old were you, Dad, when that bridge collapsed while you were you driving the tractor over it? I can't remember all the details. Would you tell us once more?"

"Mom, can you tell about . . ." and there will be another request for some other story of God's amazing intervention.

Even better, though, is when a parent can articulate how God has worked in his (or her) child's life. "Remember when you had to go to the principal's office and how God sent a little girl angel to take the sting out of that experience?"

"Remember how you became a writer in college?"

"Remember in sixth grade when you got caught . . . and God intervened before you became a juvenile delinquent?"

All these stories represent the fingerprints of God on our lives, and they're worthy of examining and reexamining with wonder and awe and faith—and of course, faith is built and strengthened with each retelling.

Keep in mind: by learning to see God's involvement in their own lives over time, parents can develop expertise at discerning God's ways in their children's lives. The opposite is equally true. Parents who have missed God's activity in their personal lives will have a more difficult challenge convincing their children that God is really involved at all.

Your family has these stories too. Reflect on the messes—those seasons of life when disorder ruled, or the dreaded fear came to pass, perhaps mayhem reigned. Then, as you mentally process the eventual outcomes, choose to ascribe to God what to this point you may have only thought of as chance or luck or coincidence. If you're just catching on to this bigger picture, then you can receive with joy that so much more is at work in your life and in your children's lives than perhaps you had realized to date. It's true: God is always at work and active in all our lives.

When we were new to this truth, we were like novice bicyclists—a little wobbly on the turns, a little too shaky in the messes. But as we became spiritually stronger, we were able to negotiate even life's sharpest of turns. What made the difference? Experience. Trust. Success. One shaky mess survived strengthens faith for the next wobbly corner to come. Soon, with enough God-experience, we are yelling back at life's messes, "You're history. You can't overtake us. We're out of here and moving on."

THE PROTECTION OF A PARENT'S FAITH

Mom Burton, Valerie's mother, had this kind of faith at the shakiest corner of their whole family's life. When she was sixty-three, Valerie's professor father turned sixty-five and chose to retire. We remember the plans they were making, and how much they were looking forward to this new stage of life. We talked together frequently about their various options. We were excited for them, as was the rest of the family, that they could finally pursue some of their postponed dreams. Valerie had a few concerns, though nothing critical.

Would they sell "my house" and move to Florida, or build a new house at the farm? Definitely they intended to be snowbirds and soak up the sun of Florida for the remainder of their lives. But two months after Dad's long-anticipated retirement, my father contracted encephalitis, which burned out his brain. He lived for four-and-a-half heartbreaking years in a vegetative state, then died without ever saying another word or recognizing any of us again.

I was twenty-six, pregnant with our first child, but any joyful anticipation was crushed by this turn in our family. My faith wavered. I alternated between being heartbroken and angry.

The memories of those years are indelible—the prayerful pleadings for God to restore our father, the fetid odor of the antiseptically clean hospitals, the blank (or worse) fearful look in his eyes, the shuffling walk and confusion in everything he tried to do—the cloud that rained grief over each of those days during that four-and-a-half year period. But overriding all those terrible memories is my mother's faith. Even though they had not planned to spend their final days together like this, even though she cried and grieved for him, she never wavered in her faith in God.

"God doesn't make mistakes, Valerie. Don't ever doubt that."

"It rains on the just and the unjust. Life is like that. This is our particular season of foul weather."

"God is in the messes."

She would find things to be grateful for: that this calamity hadn't befallen a younger man in our family; that we had wonderful health workers watching over Dad; that there was enough money to have him cared for in a nursing facility; that new babies (mine!) were bringing joy into our lives right in the midst of all this pain; that we had all experienced the kindness of strangers along the way helping us with flat tires and home repairs. On and on this gratefulness litany ministered to my doubt.

Two years after Valerie's dad's death, Mom Burton died suddenly while square dancing with friends one night. The last words she said were, "Oh, what fun!" She was engaged and six weeks away from being remarried to a lifetime family friend. Instead, we buried her next to Dad, in the dress in which she had planned to be married. The doctors said she died from a heart attack. We, her family, believe she died from joy. The pure joy—of life and love and new beginnings—was just too much for her.

Here is the most amazing thing to Valerie and me, her siblings, and our family in all of this: almost twenty years later, the essence of Mom Burton remains with us. We have been left with so much more than a house or memories, regardless of how precious. What we live and collectively breathe is her faith.

Your children too can be left with your faith. Through the years, your unwavering faith will protect, providing a shieldlike covering from life's attacks. It will comfort as well as strengthen when life seems a little too messy even for the experienced. This is your most enduring legacy, one your children can live and breathe for years.

God is with us in the messes. What a precious heritage. Believe it when you are going through your own life messes. Practice getting the wobbliness out at every life turn. Recount God's activity as you've experienced it. Tell your children those stories and the ones you've seen in their lives. Help them identify God's fingerprints in their own life messes. Build up a collective family track record of "rememberings." Doing so will help your kids learn how to take life's sharp turns.

If you follow through on what we're suggesting, you will leave your children more than a cherished family home or an estate of great worth. Help your children to see that God is in all their messes, and you will leave them with a spiritual home. God is the soul's spiritual home, but any of us can choose to live elsewhere—in doubt, in fear, in alienation. Trust in God is the spiritual heritage your children and ours will need to face the days to come. Help them learn now how to get the wobbliness out of their faith by taking those sharp life turns with confidence in God. Impress upon your kids that God is in all the messes.

When you do, you will notice that you, too, are a little stronger, a little less wobbly, a little braver, and more able to increase your speed, courage, and confidence at the corners in front of the scariest places a parent and child will ever have to travel in life.

Train a child in the way he should go, and
when he is old he will not turn from it.

—PROVERBS 22:6

7

. . . .

Lesson Seven

A CHILD'S BENT—
KEY TO A
PROMISING FUTURE

O ne of the most gratifying experiences of parenting is watching the emergence of your child's soul. To the parents with
eyes of the soul to see, this is a front-row seat to one of the
greatest shows on earth.

Here is mystery:

Where did that spiritual sensitivity come from?

Here is wonder:

*From our own flesh and blood a delightful spiritual stranger is becoming
known to us.*

Here is awe:

*This child has more than two parents. A heavenly Father is drawing near
and parenting supernaturally in places where we can't go as human parents.
Amazing!*

But sometimes parents miss these developing signs of the emerging soul, or at least fail to understand their significance. The two of
us didn't exactly miss out on all of this; it's just that we didn't fully
comprehend what we were witnessing along the way.

We now understand what was not so clear to us as younger parents: indicators appear throughout the experiences of childhood of what is to come in adulthood. All during our children's growing up years our sons were giving us hints about the men they would become. From very early on there were a variety of clues—perceptible evidences—about "the way [they] should go" (Proverbs 22:6).

Looking back from this vantage point, Valerie and I realize that these signals were there to help us direct and encourage our boys according to how God had wired each of them. In those early years, too many times we missed what today seems obvious. Because we could be so clueless, our kids sometimes lacked the spiritual encouragement needed from Dad or Mom to develop those budding tendencies or early signs of giftedness. Oh, we noticed what they did. But we were quick to place most everything in the category of *cute* or *precocious.* We just didn't know to take certain of their inclinations more seriously.

SIGNS OF THINGS TO COME

Neither of us understood (no one ever told us, as best we can remember) how a child's early spiritual leanings or interests could be linked years later to that same child's adult place in God's kingdom.

The whole process of "spiritual becoming" is so intriguing and heartening that we would hate for any parents to miss this part of their child's shaping to faith. Nor would we want any child to miss the timely parental encouragement necessary along the way to become all God has made him or her to be.

Scripture tells us to "train a child in the way he should go, and when he is old he will not turn from it" (Proverbs 22:6). It's not uncommon for Christian parents to think of this classic biblical text as a mandate to ensure that their children receive formal education about moral values and spiritual truths—and for sure, this passage would support that application. But there's more meant here than the obvious. The phrase "in the way he should go" can literally be translated "according to the child's way"—referring to the child's inclinations, inherent strengths, unique aptitude, and basic disposition—or said differently, according to his or her intrinsic bent.

In addition, this biblical mandate highlights the opportunity and responsibility of parents to provide their children with focused personal attention, doing everything possible to encourage each child to develop fully his or her God-given capacities and abilities.

And why does this matter so much? Because a child's spiritual bent can lead to the essential spiritual qualities that God will use powerfully in his or her adult years to come. It's as though, from the earliest days, God is already preparing a child's heart for the role he or she will play in His kingdom someday. These indicators of what is to come may surface exceedingly early in the life a child—so early that some parents might readily dismiss what's happening, or at best minimize these "clues" as little more than eccentrically charming behaviors.

MISSING YOUR CHILD'S SPIRITUAL BENT

One reason parents miss the initial signs of a child's emerging spirituality is because other life developments are so obvious—so much easier to grasp and observe. For instance, it's unmistakable when a child is athletically inclined or gifted. From elementary school-age on, he or she is usually picked first whenever teams are forming. Throughout the growing up years in most communities a young person with athletic prowess can be showered with attention and success. People notice the impact players for the school teams—the top scorers, the "winners," the record setters—who are receiving the trophies and walking away with all the awards. In certain locales these kids are the honored and privileged heroes.

Also, it's nearly impossible to overlook intellectual acumen in a child—especially since this is a value our culture and school systems reward so highly. Even in the early years of grade school, such a child might be put into gifted or advanced placement classes. Honor rolls and dean's lists are published in the local papers. The public acknowledgement and preferential treatment so commonly bestowed upon these high-caliber "gifted" students essentially guarantees that most everyone knows who the really smart kids are.

Those with outstanding abilities in music, acting, speaking, writing, or any other form of artistic expression—drawing, painting, sculpting, designing—all point to children whose emerging selves are blessed with abundant creativity. And likely, due to their accompanying artistic temperaments, their unique capacities could not go unnoticed even if you tried to ignore them.

But the child with a particularly sensitive spiritual bent may not be so readily detected. And because our culture as a whole seems clueless about this type of giftedness, it may be completely up to parents to pick up on and nurture these special qualities. No wonder you can easily miss your child's spiritual bent.

SIGNS OF SPIRITUAL THINGS TO COME

There's a fascinating account in the New Testament that touches on the early signs of spiritual things to come. The story begins with a set of godly parents and their remarkable child.

In Luke 1 we learn that Elizabeth and her husband, Zechariah, were good people whose lives pleased the Lord in every way possible. But they were barren and older. Then one day, without warning or expectation, an angel suddenly appeared to Zechariah. Zechariah's immediate response? The Bible says "he was startled and was gripped with fear" (verse 12)—yet another version of an adult reaction to "angels in the halls." (Remember Zane in chapter 5?)

The angel spoke directly to him with this wonderful news:

> Do not be afraid, Zechariah; your prayer has been heard. Your wife Elizabeth will bear you a son, and you are to give him the name John. He will be a joy and delight to you, and many will rejoice because of his birth, for he will be great in the sight of the Lord. . . . He will be filled with the Holy Spirit even *from birth*. Many of the people of Israel will he bring back to the Lord their God. And he will go on before the Lord, in the spirit and power of Elijah, to turn the hearts of the fathers to their children and the disobedient to the wisdom of the righteous—to make ready a people prepared for the Lord. (verses 13–17, italics added)

Then, exactly as the angel predicted, Elizabeth became pregnant. But before this child, John—later known as John the Baptist—was born, a very interesting thing happened. Mary, who had received her own angelic visitor and by now was carrying Jesus in her womb, "got ready and hurried" to visit Elizabeth (verse 39). Upon entering Zechariah's home, Mary greeted Elizabeth. And at that moment Elizabeth's baby "leaped in her womb"—or in Elizabeth's own words, "As soon as the sound of your greeting reached my ears, the baby in my womb leaped for joy" (verse 44).

Try to envision this—prenatal John, encased in his mother's womb but straining to unfold from his fetal position to dance with joy in the presence of the Lord! The angel declared, "He will be filled with the Holy Spirit even from birth," or as the CEV puts it, "The power of the Holy Spirit will be with him from the time he is born." If the angel's words seemed like an exceptionally early sign of spirituality, then what do we make of fetal John dancing, somersaulting, and exploding with happy recognition of the presence of the fetal Son of God?

WHAT WAS THREE-YEAR-OLD JOHN LIKE?

John had an incredibly powerful impact on people. The Bible records that he was a "joy and delight" to his parents and that "many [rejoiced] because of his birth." Think of it: as a three-year-old, John the Baptist was also filled with the power of the Holy Spirit. *What was that like?* we wonder. *And how would you expect a Spirit-filled toddler going through the "terrible twos" to behave? Who can even guess?!*

The Bible explains that John helped people think straight—"to think as they ought" (verse 17 CEV)—and to obey God. In fact, "because of John, parents will be more thoughtful of their children," the CEV Bible notes. Suppose that only happened during his preaching and baptizing years, or could it also have been occurring some throughout his childhood? Scripture makes it explicit that from John's birth—and even before—he had an unusually high sensitivity to the Spirit of God. From the very beginning he influenced his peers for good. He was a child of exceptional character. He was a kid who lived straighter than the other boys. Perhaps he was the kind of kid who even dared to challenge the adults in his world to think straight. Probably some, we suspect, were put off with this kind of spiritual precocity from someone lower on the age chain.

John the Baptist would "turn the hearts of the fathers to their children and the disobedient to the wisdom of the righteous—to make ready a people prepared for the Lord." Could he have been but twelve when that kind of healing power began to be noticed on the family structures around him? Might he have waited until his sixteenth birthday before he started to dress differently from the other children? Suppose he held on until he was at least twenty to say good-bye to his parents (making them empty nesters) so he could move to the desert where, the gospel of Luke explains, he lived and prepared his soul for the ministry of readying the world for the coming of the Redeemer? All we're specifically told is that as John grew up, he "became strong in spirit" (verse 80), or as the *Contemporary English Version* puts it, "God's Spirit gave him great power."

We can only speculate on the specific early indicators or signs in the life of this unique man of God who was to come. We do know that John the Baptist's essential spiritual qualities as an adult included all of these characteristics mentioned in the text, and certainly more. He would prepare the way of the Lord as none other before or after. And Scripture is extraordinarily precise that very early in John's life—from birth, even from before birth—there were signs of the unique spiritual role he would play in God's kingdom.

WHEN WE ENCOURAGE OUR CHILDREN'S EARLY SPIRITUAL INTERESTS . . .

Did John's parents, Zechariah and Elizabeth, fully understand what was going on in the unfolding life of their young son? We'd venture to guess they had to have their moments of doubt and confusion, wondering where all of this was really headed. But based on the historical record in Luke's gospel, and to their credit, these parents were unusually sensitive when it came to matters of the soul. Their little boy's intrinsic spiritual bent was obviously noticed and—evidenced by the eventual outcomes—was most likely encouraged throughout all of his growing up years. Watching over the emerging soul of their child was, indeed, their most strategic parental assignment of all.

When spiritually sensitive adults encourage a child's emerging spirituality, wonderful things can happen. As a result, the world may never be the same.

Our pastor, Bill Hybels, told of an epiphany in his own emerging faith that, fortunately, was handled with great sensitivity by an adult. His second grade teacher was reading a story to her classroom about the young boy Samuel hearing the voice of God:

"I'm sitting in the class, listening to the teacher talk about how God can speak to people. And the other kids are throwing paper wads and fooling around. But my heart is beating fast because I'm sitting there thinking, *I can identify with that, because I think I have felt God speak to me.*

"I had a sense, even at that age when I was about to do something wrong, it was as if God would speak to me and say, 'Oh, Bill, you don't want to do that.' Or sometimes I felt Him telling me to do something right. We had some physically challenged children at our school. Sometimes the other kids would gang up on them. I can remember very clearly God saying, 'You stand up for these disabled kids. You stand in the way. Take a beating if you have to. Don't ever let somebody mistreat someone who is hurting that way.'

"So I was thinking about all of this and all of the other kids filed out for recess, but I stayed behind. Very timidly I walked up to the teacher's desk and asked, 'Do you think God still talks to little boys today?' It was a very vulnerable question. I think back on it and realize that if she had mishandled that situation, the whole trajectory of my life could have been changed.

"She said, 'Billy, I think God does speak to little boys. And I think God would even speak to you if you kept your heart open.' And I asked, 'Well, how do you do that?' She dug in her desk and handed me a poem, explaining, 'I'm going to challenge you to memorize this poem. It might take you a while, but I think if you memorized it, it will get in your head and serve you well. When you get it memorized, come back and you can say it for me.'"

So Billy took it home. And he did not come back in a week. He memorized it that night. "I memorized it so thoroughly that it has become a part of my life and a part of my understanding of spiritual life," he says. In fact, Hybels has reviewed the poem "thousands of times" throughout his Christian life.

Oh give me Samuel's ear.
An open ear, O Lord.

Alive and quick to hear each whisper of Thy word.
Like him to answer to Thy call.
And to obey Thee first of all.

Hybels concludes: "The foundational stone of my spiritual life was laid that day. I started believing that God would talk to me throughout my day."[1]

What an amazing testimonial. The responses of spiritually sensitive adults really do matter when asked heartfelt questions by little boys and girls! Who could have imagined that, some forty years later, the senior pastor of a thriving ministry like Willow Creek Community Church would reflect on an experience he had as a seven-year-old and say, "The foundational stone of my spiritual life was laid that day."

This is not simply a story about spiritual precocity, or spiritual giftedness showing early in a future leader's life. It is much more. It is testimony to the seal of God on a young boy's heart that would set a tone of openness to God even into adulthood. These are early signs of what is to come. They need to be noticed, encouraged, and developed by caring and sensitive adults.

SIGNS OF THINGS THAT ARE AND WILL BE

Whether or not your child will grow up like Bill Hybels to be a nationally known ministry leader who's impacting his entire generation, who can say? But be certain of this: If your child demonstrates an early sensitivity to God—an openness to hear, see, and experience Him—God may be setting a relational seal in his or her heart that will last throughout your child's lifetime. And you, Mom and Dad, won't want to miss that for anything!

How wonderful to catch the bent of a child's developing soul. She loves to pray? Watch out, world. A prayer warrior is down on her knees and she's only five! He talks to all of his friends about Jesus? Keep an eye on that one—someday we might be taking our seeker friends to hear him speak because of his gifts of evangelism and preaching. She sings out her heart to God all the time? There may be a soul-impacting worship leader in the making. He has more faith than we do sometimes? What mountain do you suppose he'll be moving in future days? Likely something no one else would even try. She wants to give her toys to children who don't have any? What will she be giving away when she's older and actually has something? He feels sad for other people? Mercy, sweet mercy is forming in this kid. Maybe God is preparing your child's heart to set the prisoners free and bind up the brokenhearted (see Isaiah 61:1).

These are all early signs of God's kingdom plans for a child's life. But it's not just about the future—it's also about today.

Sometimes parents understand this dynamic better by taking a look back at what was playing out in their child's life. "*Now* we get it . . . so that's what that was all about," parents exclaim. We can relate.

"I WANT TO MAKE AFRICA RICH"

After Brendan entered middle school, he announced one day that he wanted "to make Africa rich." We didn't have a clue about what God was forming in our son's soul. We just didn't "get" it. But fortunately, God stopped our mouths from telling Brendan that that was an *impossible* job. Instead, we watched as he developed a plan "to make Africa rich." He and his best friend, Rich, organized their friends into a bicycle brigade to distribute Lucite collection boxes from World Relief at stores all around our town. Every week they collected the donations and turned them in to World Relief's nearby headquarters. It was all very organized and, we thought, well, kind of cute.

But we would be amazed to watch this plan grow beyond the cute stage in our eleven-year-old's life. When the Lucite boxes seemed too small a dent in the "let's make Africa rich" scheme, they moved to a new strategy—a strategy that was more sacrificial and required tremendous discipline on their part. They began approaching adults—relatives, parents of their friends, our personal friends, people at church, coaches, teachers—to match the money they could personally save from odd jobs, allowances, etc. This meant any personal spending for them, for the year or so that this went on, would cost their mission many times that! We were both proud and touched to see these two boys working so diligently and sacrificially for a cause that was far beyond them.

When some key leaders in the adult world heard about the efforts of these two boys, Brendan and Rich were even asked to speak in a couple of churches to share their heart and plans for Africa. Some special offerings were taken for their projects. Over a couple of years, several thousand dollars were raised "to make Africa rich."

It was an *Aha . . . so that's what this child is about!* experience for the two of us. Brendan's soul was forming before our eyes—shaping to the possibilities of enormous faith someday—and we had a thrilling front-row seat.

Here's the thing: he never succeeded in "making Africa rich"—or you would have heard about it by now! But looking back, we realize that what was emerging in our son all along was a spiritual gift of mercy. All the signs were there. He had a predisposition to make friends with kids who were not considered to be part of the "popular crowd." We have to admit, some of them were *more* than a little strange. His middle school principal actually dubbed him "Saint Brendan" because of this tendency to care about and collect kids no one else liked. Wounded or stray animals often lived under our porch and in our bushes. How did they know to find this kid? The mercy that radiated from him attracted them like a magnet!

Today, Brendan is a grown young man. And although he's not making Africa rich, he has become a professional therapist at a Christian counseling center. And while he's building his private practice, on the side he works at a behavioral hospital—a "holding bin" for kids in trouble with the law, kids who are sexual offenders, kids no one can do *anything* with. This is definitely not the "popular crowd." But he loves this work. His mercy gifts are fully engaged with these challenging kids. What would drain most adults energizes him. Looking back, the signs were always there. *Now* we get it! The seemingly odd pieces of this puzzle were faith shaping all along.

We've had those *Aha . . . so that's what this kid is all about!* moments with both of our sons. We still laugh at a certain family video taken when Justin was barely four. He is playing soccer with the older kids, or *trying* to play soccer with them, but they're completely ignoring him. He throws a fit, stomping around the yard. Funny stuff! But the next thing you see, Justin is in their faces—telling them what to do, how to play, and why they should listen to him! But did we, his parents, get it? No. We thought it was pure, raw, naughty-boy bossiness. But with a backward glance that taped incident was telling us something. It was an early indicator of his unfolding spiritual gift of leadership—awkwardly and inappropriately expressed, yes, but there just the same.

The signs were always there in Justin's life. He hung out with older kids with a certain amount of influence. And what he lacked in saintliness, he definitely made up for in the "being-in-charge" department. He has just graduated from college and due to a regular column he wrote in the school paper, one in which he challenged the direction of the college and the majority-accepted opinions, we had been praying, "O God, please just get him graduated before he leads a coup to take over the school and gets kicked out!" Phew! We're glad that's over. But someday, with a backward look this experience, too, will be a piece of his emerging spiritual bent. We will probably say, "Aha . . . we knew it!" The signs were there all along the way.

A BIG-TIME GIVER
GETS HIS START WITH A NICKEL

My (Steve's) brother-in-law, Daryle Doden, has a natural knack for business. That bent could have been discerned as early as age seven, when he sold garden vegetables in order to purchase his first bicycle, or perhaps during junior high school, when he started an odd-job service. Those childhood business endeavors were an early glimpse of future success: at age twenty-six he began a rebar sales business that has since grown to become the largest independent concrete reinforcing bar fabricator and distributor in America.

Perhaps less obvious in those early years was his gift of giving, nurtured by his father, which has allowed him to give millions in support of Christian causes around the world. He once explained how his father influenced him. This is a terrific example of a dad who was not "clueless" but spiritually sensitive to his child's emerging faith patterns.

"Years ago someone asked me how I overcame my poverty-stricken roots to becoming a successful businessman. The question took me somewhat by surprise. I never saw myself as poor. I guess that was primarily because of my father. He believed that he served a God of unlimited resources. My father taught us that if we wanted something and God wanted us to have it, that He would see that we got it. My only frustration as a child with this philosophy was that my father, being a man of simple faith, did not want the same things that I did!

"It was this theology that caused my father to be a giving man. Although he never made more than eighty-five dollars a week as a country pastor—less than the wage of the average production worker —he always tithed and was consistently one of the first in our community to give to a worthy cause.

"When I was about four years old my father gave me my first allowance—a nickel. I remember his instructions very clearly, 'Daryle, you are old enough now to have an allowance. I will give you a nickel each week. Now a penny out of every two nickels belongs to God as a tithe—so the first week a penny of that nickel should go into the church offering. The second week you can decide whether or not you would like to give an offering to God.'

"A short time after I began receiving this newfound wealth, my father challenged his little country flock to raise $1,200 for a Jeep needed by some missionaries in the Ozark Mountains. I remember the excitement of going with my father to the big city of Indianapolis to pick up the vehicle. We parked it in the parking lot with a bucket hung on the door for people to give. It was thrilling to see the coins and bills fill the bucket until the time was announced that we had met the goal.

"His example made giving seem as natural as breathing. As a child I often pledged my allowance to support missionaries, people in need, and other projects. But when I was eleven, God gave me a new source of funding for my interest in giving. I had been praying that God would give me a paper route so I could earn money for college. I promised I would commit three dollars per week to God if He would help me get a paper route that paid at least ten dollars a week.

"But God would have to help me get a route because normally a kid would have to be a substitute carrier for years to be in line for his own route.

"Shortly before committing my problem to God, I had asked the twin brothers who delivered papers in my neighborhood if I could have their route. They said I could, but that they would not be quitting for years. Then I began praying.

"A short time later, most likely just to be pesky, I asked again. I couldn't believe their answer! They said I could have their route because they were quitting to baby-sit for their new brother. Since there were two of them, they did not have a substitute carrier to whom they were obligated. God blessed beyond what I ever expected. Not only did He provide me with my own route, but He provided one that paid thirteen dollars a week, leaving me with ten dollars net after fulfilling my promise to God.

"These childhood lessons of God's goodness and faithfulness have remained with me to this day. It is with great joy and blessing that God allows me to continue to have the means to give to Him."

Watching Daryle through the years has made us marvel at the resourcefulness of God. To take what started as a nickel tithe and to build that spiritual bent in a young boy's heart until today literally millions of dollars have been produced to help kingdom causes—including, yes, even enriching the continent of Africa—is God at His creative best!

SEEING OUR CHILDREN'S POTENTIAL, NOT THEIR SHORTCOMINGS

But sometimes parents have a hard time seeing a child through the spiritual potential grid. Parents are more apt to focus on a child's weaknesses and shortcomings that are a concern currently or could later pose a problem.

So it has always been. The Old Testament tells the story of an overlooked child of great spiritual possibilities. Samuel, well into his adult years by now—the same Samuel who heard God calling him as a young boy—heard God instructing him to go visit Jesse of Bethlehem. God told Samuel that He had chosen one of Jesse's sons to replace Saul as the next king of Israel. And so the prophet Samuel watched as Jesse brought seven sons, one by one, to pass in front of him. But Samuel, as was his practice as a child, was still sensitively listening to God's voice.

He said to the father, "'The LORD has not chosen these. . . . Are these all the sons you have?'

"'There is still the youngest,' Jesse answered, 'but he is tending the sheep.'

"Samuel said, 'Send for him; we will not sit down until he arrives'" (1 Samuel 16:10–11). Jesse cooperated, but the text clearly implies that he was reluctant at best.

What was going through the parental side of Jesse's mind that edited his son David out of the running for king? Did he think him too young? Did he consider him too odd, too different, from the rest of his boys to even have a shot? Perhaps he wondered how a sensitive kid like David, who loved to play the harp, could ever grow up to become a strong enough man to lead armies into battle someday. And his preoccupation with that crazy slingshot—what's up with that? Or maybe David's redheaded temperament worried his dad? Who knows?

But when David arrived, the Lord said to Samuel, "Rise and anoint him; he is the one" (verse 12). And so Samuel, listening to God, saw things in this young boy that David's own father had completely missed. The Bible says "from that day on the Spirit of the LORD came upon David in power" (verse 13).

There's no question that this encounter with Samuel caused Jesse to see David in a whole new light. Perhaps, for the first time, Jesse was beginning to get the bigger picture that though this youngest son was different, his unique abilities and unusual interests were God given, a part of God's plans that needed to be affirmed, explored, and developed.

SEEING OUR CHILDREN THROUGH OTHERS' EYES

Seeing your children through another person's eyes helps most of us dads and moms get a better perspective. One of our biggest *Aha . . . so that's what this kid is about!* moments was experienced when someone wiser and with more emotional distance from the situation helped us get a clearer point of view on our son Brendan.

Go back with us to the third grade. We were scheduled for a regular parent-teacher conference with his homeroom teacher. Stories from earlier chapters have already established that he was well behaved and usually received glowing reports from school. But we had seen other things in this son that worried us. He had a tendency to be spacey—preoccupied with his own creative inner world. He was tested as gifted, but in third grade he still wasn't reading much. Brendan was an adorable child, but school just didn't seem to be taking. We were concerned parents.

During our parent-teacher conference that afternoon with Mrs. Mears, his teacher, she told us what class was like with Brendan every day—which caused us to move from *concerned* to *alarmed*. "Every day," she informed us, "when it's time to line up for lunch, all the other children rush to get ready; but Brendan doesn't budge. He stays involved in his own project at his desk. Then every day, when he finally looks up at the other children standing in line for lunch, he asks, 'Where are we going?' "

Our hearts sank. Valerie had been a schoolteacher for years. She knew how hard it was to have a child who wasn't a part of the group process in the classroom. "Oh, I am so sorry. That must be very frustrating for you," she said to Mrs. Mears.

"No, Mr. and Mrs. Bell, I am not telling you this because I'm frustrated with Brendan. I want you to understand your son. He has such a rich interior world that he hardly needs the structure of school to keep himself occupied or motivated. Whatever's going on inside his mind, it's just too wonderful to stop to bother to line up for lunch, or learn to read, or any of the other things he views as mundane in the course of a school day."

She explained to us what we couldn't see or understand ourselves. She saw a wonderful side to him, positive qualities that we had overlooked because of our worry. And she was right. She gave us a viewpoint on our son that helped us see that he was (and is) special. Finally, after several years of trying to understand this kid, in fourth grade Brendan decided it might be advantageous to learn how to read. And that year he went from the lowest reading group to the highest. He now tells us that he didn't bother learning to read earlier because it just hadn't seemed very important or interesting to him until then. Mrs. Mears was right about that too!

TREASURES IN JARS OF CLAY

Hmm . . . kids can be such mysteries to their parents. What has been entrusted to your care? What little human puzzle are you trying

127

to figure out? Maybe God is investing gifts in the soul of your child that you are only beginning to understand. The signs are already there in many cases. We have this treasure of God's light and glory in the "jars of clay" (2 Corinthians 4:7) of our children. We just need to develop spiritual eyes that can see such things, hone the spiritual sensitivity to encourage such things, and savor the wonder to realize how awesomely creative God's ways are in the heart of a child.

Somewhere in this world today, a little boy is learning to listen to God's voice. In the future God will speak to him clearly and often. And when that man listens and obeys, the world may never be the same.

Somewhere in this world today, a child holds a sweaty little nickel—peso, franc, yen, or pound—in his clasped hand, and many years from now that small amount of money will miraculously grow and multiply into millions available to missions and ministries that will help "to make Africa rich."

Somewhere in this world tonight, a child is tucked into bed exploring a rich interior world that when more fully developed will produce the inspiring novel or awesome painting or remarkable piece of sculpting that will elevate hearts to a higher moral consciousness and challenge people across the globe to live more spiritually productive lives.

Somewhere in this world, at this very moment under a parent's care, these kids are on their way to becoming great men and women of God. These "jars of clay" look like children now. But beyond the chubby cheeks and empty-toothed grins, beyond the knobby knees and scraped elbows there are other signs—signs of the places these kids are created to play in the kingdom of God.

Don't miss this one, Dad and Mom. Look closely at your children. We have this glorious treasure in precious small jars of clay. Their unique bent, emerging before your very eyes, could be the key to a promising future that could change the world.

NOTE

1. Bill Hybels, "Leadings in the Life of a God-honoring Leader," message delivered at The Leadership Summit, Willow Creek Community Church, Barrington, Ill., 10 August 1996.

I rejoiced with those who said to me,
"Let us go to the house of the LORD."

· · · · · · ·

—PSALM 122:1

YOU'VE GOTTA LOVE THE CHURCH!

We love the church. When we try to think of what our lives would have been like without the community of faith, one word comes to mind: *impoverished.* We have been lifted by her worship, softened by her prayers, comforted by her mercies, ministered to by her music, made wiser by her teachers, challenged to be caring by her preachers, and motivated to be productive by her leaders. Most of all, we have been joined by others in enduring relationships who also see life through the same spiritual grid we do.

We are rich in community. We are rich in faith. Spiritual wealth is our greatest treasure.

Our sons, now young adults, seem to have caught this same passion. But admittedly it has been an acquired taste. Even though we strongly expressed the value that we are not "Lone Ranger" Christians, that we belong to a wider community of faith and therefore participate in its shared life, our kids occasionally didn't see it like that.

Complaints like, "Youth group is so boring. Dad, Mom, please don't make me go this week," were sometimes heard at our house, especially during the middle school years. They were quickly followed by a parental response something like, "Sorry. No passes on this one. If it's boring, you'll just have to get on the solution side and try to find a way to make it more interesting."

Complaints about the church consistently bumped into a parental "no fly" zone in our home. Because we highly value belonging to the community of faith, we didn't want our sons to miss this in their own lives. We learned to be immovable. Church involvement was a nonnegotiable.

WILL OUR CHILDREN MAKE A DIFFERENCE?

Looking back, we recognize that our admonition to "make it better" was more than a direction to stay engaged. In some part of our hearts we also wanted our sons to take leadership, to plug in their giftedness and impact their own smaller communities of faith. We were eager for them to learn early on that their lives can make a difference—or should we say *must* make a difference.

Whenever we teach parenting, we talk about this family value. We say, "We did not want to send wounders into the world; we wanted to send healers. Our hearts' desire, the lifelong direction of our prayers, has been for our sons to be problem solvers or leaders in their own generation of the church."

The response? It's interesting. We hear the same audience reaction nearly every time. There's an audible collective sigh—like a community-of-faith longing that passes in sync from the heart through the lungs—a deep, shared yearning that wordlessly declares, "Amen . . . Us too . . . That's what we want for our kids as well."

We want our kids' lives to matter for the kingdom, to make a difference, to be the ones who step up to the challenge and give their lives to a great cause.

We're guessing you do too. Most likely, that's one of the reasons you're reading this book.

WHAT DO KIDS GET OUT OF CHURCH, ANYWAY?

Christianity is a community faith. Spiritual formation is more effective when other believers hold us to a level of accountability, insisting we get it right. Spiritual passion is caught as much as it is taught. You just can't get to the same depth of commitment watching church on television. It is in community where we learn that we belong, and we matter. It is also in community that we learn that other people matter and have a need to belong as well.

There are so many reasons to "do church." But the reasons for kids to do church are even more significant. It's especially important for kids.

For one thing, church is a place where kids experience belonging —belonging to one's own family and to a larger family of community.

My earliest memories are connected to church. To this day I (Steve) can scroll my memory for several snapshots of church belonging that are vividly intact from my childhood. One of my earliest memories was when I was three. I clearly remember being held by my father, who was standing in the back of the church sanctuary. The congregation was singing:

Give me oil in my lamp, keep me burning;
Give me oil in my lamp, I pray.
Give me oil in my lamp, keep me burning, burning, burning;
Keep me burning 'til the break of day.
Sing hosanna, sing hosanna, sing hosanna to the King of Kings;
Sing hosanna, sing hosanna, sing hosanna to the King.

I was singing too, with heart and soul—and with all the volume my little lungs could let it rip! For sure, I was oblivious to the meaning of the song (actually, I'm not so certain I could explain it all that well today), but what I do clearly remember is an irresistible sense of joy—and acceptance. All during the singing of "Give Me Oil in My Lamp" the people in the congregation kept turning around and smiling at me. Wrapped in my father's arms, the focus of his embarrassed laughter, I felt protected and encouraged. I didn't realize why at the time, but I did feel noticed and most of all very loved.

Church children often have these experiences of being cherished, celebrated, and having a sense of belonging. There's nothing like the church! We didn't want our kids to miss that.

As far back as I can remember, I looked forward to going to church. I felt special there. It was like home away from home. Though it was a large church for our town—about five hundred attended—it was very personal and friendly. People knew my name. It was a fun place to go—I loved being with my friends, hearing the stories, singing the songs, competing in Bible drills—there was always lots of laughter in the church where I was raised. I belonged to this community family. I was secure.

Then one Christmas season, they showed me just how much I mattered. It was a small thing in some ways, but a sacrifice just the same. That Christmas, before I was even old enough to go to school, I broke out in a horrible rash following the children's Christmas program at church. On the church platform, I had been standing close to the large Christmas tree. After some tests the doctor determined that I had a serious allergy to freshly cut pine. From that point forward (until I was a teenager) the church banned using live Christmas trees—just because of me! I learned very quickly that I mattered at church. Those people authentically cared about my well-being. I was one of those "little ones welcomed in Jesus' name" (see Matthew 18:5), and that welcome made a lasting imprint on my soul. Oh, that church would be like this for all people!

The community of faith in my home church played a significant role in shaping my life during the teenage years as well. Many of the adults in our church were like extended family to me. In junior high school I remember declaring to my parents, "You know, I really have *five* moms when you think about it. Mom, you're number one; Norma Bate (my best friend's mom) is number two; Aunt BeBe (my cousin's mom) is number three; Aunt Irene (my dad's sister) is number four; and Janet McCracken (the pastor's wife) is number five. I guess if something ever happens to you, Mom, you won't have to worry about me!" I can't recall if she took any comfort in that thought or not.

The point is, during those growing up years I felt incredibly connected and secure because of the varied and healthy relationships that were maintained through our wider community of faith.

If it's true, as some experts say, that the central issue for this generation of children is belonging, then we all need to look at the church with a fresh set of eyes. We need to understand the kind of belonging that church can offer to kids. For a generation of kids who have found connectedness outside of family and outside of church, we need to offer the special belonging that only a spiritual family of faith can provide.

There is nothing like the church—especially when it communicates, "You matter to God, and let us show you just how much!"

CHURCH: A PLACE WHERE
KIDS AND ADULTS CAN "GET A GRIP"

When I (Valerie) think about what our kids need to stay balanced in life, I take that factor—the church—and multiply it by ten for my own adult life. Church helps me keep my life in perspective. If kids need spiritual help, sometimes we adults need the attention of heaven's entire emergency room. Case in point. Not long ago a girlfriend, Ginger, telephoned me and suggested that we enter into an accountability relationship to try to lose weight together. *OK. Other people are noticing. It must be time to get serious about this.*

Since I had been unable to hold myself accountable in this area, I headed into this arrangement with great enthusiasm and an empty notebook. What happened next was unexpected. I didn't conquer food. Instead, I became obsessed with food. What had been an idle interest now became my passion in life, my reason for existence. Specifically, I craved chocolate! Dark chocolate. Milk chocolate. Chocolate covered raisins. Chocolate covered peanuts. Chocolate covered . . . anything!

One morning two candy bars materialized in our home. Around lunch I began to bargain with myself. *They're only 250 calories. You'd eat that much for lunch. Why don't you just skip lunch and enjoy it?*

That's exactly what I did. I ate it and enjoyed every fat-laden, calorie-packed morsel. But not long after lunch I began to think about the other candy bar—which I found myself eating as well. The sugar high was disappointing; it wore off before the last bite was swallowed. *Oh, no, now I have to tell Ginger that I ate, not only one candy bar but two! Okay, tubby, you better get walking!*

My lack of discipline had left me in a snit. I walked and threw toward heaven my disgust and self-loathing.

God, I am a sick woman. I have a sick relationship with food. How can I help anyone else when I can't even help myself? I am totally, utterly, completely hopeless!

My journey into substance abuse and self-abuse was not over, however.

Starbucks is just a few blocks from our home. I learned that day that it is within easy walking distance.

A café mocha (chocolate, of course!) has been known to make a person feel better—at least for a while.

And so there I was, sitting in Starbucks nursing a café mocha and an ever-growing sense of self-disgust when a young woman came up to me. All the seats were taken except for the one at my table.

I barely glanced at her. "Please, sit down. You can have a seat at my table," I managed to offer despite my decidedly foul mood.

"Oh, no," she replied, "I don't want to bother you."

Bother me? How ironic. If she knew what a snit I was in she'd avoid me like the plague! I'm so bothered, how could she make things any worse?

But instead I said, "Oh, please sit down. You really won't bother me."

She hesitated and then sat down. Her name was Anna, she said. I wasn't paying much attention. I soon learned why she thought she might *bother* me.

From a shopping bag she pulled a whole head of lettuce and quartered it. Then dumping an entire bottle of yellow mustard on top she finished this concoction by sprinkling perhaps twenty bags of NutraSweet over it all. None of it had any food value whatsoever.

We began to talk. She told me she was homeless—and it was at that moment I saw her. I mean, I really took her in. She was young, maybe only thirty. She was beautiful. She was also incredibly thin. I knew I was watching a slow death in process. My heart broke.

"Now, Valerie," I heard a familiar inner voice prod. "Talk to Me about being hopeless. Talk to Me about having a sick relationship to food."

I felt shame to see my thoughts of just a few minutes past materialized in this young woman. "Oh, God, those are such terrible words! I would never say that about this young woman. She's so much more than just a woman who has a sick relationship to food. I would never call her hopeless. She's not a disease, or a lost cause—she's precious to You."

"Valerie," the same gentle inner voice said. "I wasn't talking about Anna. I was talking about you. Why do you talk about yourself like

136

that? Why are you so rough on yourself when you would never treat another person so badly? Are you really hopeless? Or are you more? Are you a woman who has a sick relationship to food only? Or are you more? Are you disgusting or loved?"

"Valerie," He might as well have said, "get a grip!"

Why do I tell this story? For the same reason that when my kids ask, "Do I have to go to church?" I say, "Absolutely!" Listen and get the point of this story. God will *rarely* show up for you or me at Starbucks. We really can't count on Starbucks for an encounter with God. But God *does* regularly meet us at church. Every week, if we are receptive, can be a God encounter.

It was in church I received the "green light" to marry Steve. It was in church that my deepest wounds have been soothed. It was in church I learned and experienced so much about God.

Though meaningful at the time, my one God encounter in Starbucks fades compared to the hundreds of life-changing, eye-opening, life-affirming encounters with God that I have had in church.

Regularly, dependably, supernaturally, God and I, God and you, meet at church. That's why we go with a sense of keen anticipation.

We can say to our children, "Go to church!" And when they ask "Why?" we can answer, "Because God will meet you there!" Really, He will. He's a regular there every week!

Am I thinking a little too highly of myself? Then in church I am both humbled and lifted up, admonished and encouraged, given the truth about who I am that also includes a huge dose of hope.

As adults and as parents, be at church and watch as God breaks through with His love—whether it's someone's arm around the shoulder that offers you belonging, or it's a song that brings tears to your eyes because it feels like it could have been written for you. It could be the Scripture that connects in a deep part of your soul or just a comment before a prayer that draws you in as if the prayer were only for you.

That's how God meets us in church. Delightfully, regularly, specifically, personally. We need to learn to "do church" with the kind of expectancy that believes God can and will touch us deeply, profoundly, and personally. And we need to help our children learn that church is where they too will encounter God.[1]

Children aren't too young to need that kind of spiritual balance in life. They need grounding. They need the bigger picture, the eternal perspective. Kids are dealing with so much that may seem trivial to adults who have forgotten how hormones and inexperience can combine in near lethal dosages. But their spiritual life can keep bad hair days, disappointing report cards, sports losses, friendship betrayals, zits, poundage, body images, and fashion changes in perspective.

Guess what? The very best place to get this kind of grounding—and a great place for your children to meet God—is in church, in the community of faith.

Church offers mission for the self-absorbed, a reason for meaningful existence for the unfocused, and a clear view of what really matters in the long run for the shortsighted.

There's nothing like the church to give a kid or a parent a grip in life! And there's no place like church to meet God.

CHURCH: A PLACE WHERE
KIDS LEARN TO CELEBRATE SPIRITUAL LIFE

Another strategic reason to "do church" is for the value of group celebration—no one can throw a party or celebrate like the church can. Worship is best when we experience it in community. Sure, every individual believer can (and should) lift his or her voice in private praise to God. Our heavenly Father wants us to—and it's always appropriate! But what can replicate or surpass the dynamic of God's power at work among us when scores, hundreds, or even thousands of voices join together in heartfelt celebratory heavenward praise? While collectively lifting our voices to God with abandon, you can be sure the children present are soaking it in with a renewed realization that they are not alone in this adventure called faith. And this is a valuable message for children to grasp.

In the early seventies, there were two guys in our youth ministry I'll never forget. Each was from a totally secular home, but within a few weeks of each other, both of them, Bill and Bob, had dramatic conversion experiences. In light of their checkered pasts, as they each began to mature in their newfound faith, their lives were being radically transformed. We were thrilled to watch what was unfolding before our very eyes.

A number of months passed, then Valerie and I decided to take a select group of students with us, including Bill and Bob, to attend InterVarsity's Urbana Missions Conference. More than eighteen thousand students from around the world descended upon the University of Illinois campus for several days of worship and training. We were totally unprepared for the impact those few days would make in the lives of these two fairly new believers. When we walked into that packed Assembly Hall arena, took our seats, and began to worship, with backup bands and worship leaders lifting our hearts and voices in corporate praise to God—they were blown away!

Until that point, they had assumed that this spiritual journey they had begun, this newfound faith in God they were now a part of, had only been "discovered" by a few of us in a student group in a South Florida church. They had no idea how many others were with them on a parallel lifetime adventure. What a forceful and timely impact this experience had on shaping their emerging faith. The power of the wider community of faith in corporate celebration builds faith—especially in young people.

Don't let your kids miss this one!

WATER CELEBRATIONS!

Among the many grand events that will cause our children to see celebration as part of the Christian faith is water baptism. They will watch happy faces and serious faces and hear great testimonies of commitment and trust—and, if they are believers never baptized, they may even participate. For the past several summers our home church, Willow Creek Community Church, has a baptismal celebration that in one afternoon baptizes over one thousand new believers. (OK, it *is* a large church.) Besides the impressive numbers, this baptismal service is a sight for other reasons as well. It is a celebration unlike any we've ever experienced. As many as twenty leaders—pastors and elders—will line the shallow waters of the campus lake. Families and friends and thousands of other interested members of the church gather on the knolls with picnic baskets, lawn chairs, babies, grandmas and grandpas, and video cameras.

For several hours, they stream down to the water to be baptized. They are not alone. They are accompanied by family members, special friends, small groups, mentors, disciplers—and the people who have been involved in helping them come to faith in Christ. Now it is their turn to make a public declaration about being a Christ follower. The group does not stop at the water's edge. All go into the water together. A small circle surrounds the one to be baptized. This is a sight! We've watched entire families embrace each other side by side, and be immersed together. Couples are sometimes "double-dunked" as they wrap arms around each other and together proclaim to the witnessing world their new lives in Christ. Wives cry tears of joy as long-prayed-for husbands take their turn in the waters. Parents of former prodigals pinch themselves. You can guess their journeys by the stories on their faces.

A few words and smiles are exchanged between the pastors and the one being baptized. "We couldn't imagine heaven without you!" "Welcome to the kingdom!" "Never forget that you matter to God!" "Do you understand what you are doing today?" "In the name of the Father, the Son, and the Holy Spirit . . ." and then down they go. Each dripping wet congregant emerges to a barrage of tears, hugs, kisses, and high fives from their we're-in-this-water-together friends. There is splashing and laughing and arms raised in praise and victory to the heavens. Cheers and applause swell from the banks where the congregation sits and celebrates one who has "come out of the closet" with his or her faith, so to speak.

But what is on each wet face—young or old, married or single, surrounded by many or accompanied by one, whatever their race or gender, regardless of their past or history—is unmistakable.

It's pure, raw joy!

When the church celebrates spiritual life, whether it's in worship, or sharing communion, or listening to someone's coming-to-faith story and responding with affirmation, well, there is no other party like it on the face of the earth—anywhere!

Don't let your kids miss this joy, this spiritual high, this worship as one corporate body.

CHURCH: A PLACE WHERE
KIDS CAN TRY OUT THEIR WINGS

We confess. Every spring we occasionally look at each other and roll our eyes a little. "Oh no, here's another one. Another kid trying to raise money for a short-term summer missions trip. Do you even *know* who this kid is?" one of us may say to the other.

The form letter typically begins:

Dear (which is already preprinted) and then obviously in their own handwriting—*Mr. and Mrs. Bell,*

(Back to preprinted text:) *I am writing to tell you about a great experience I hope to participate in this summer. During two weeks in the month of June* (or July or August) *my youth group will be working in rural Mississippi* (or Mexico or the Bahamas or Tunisia) *for "Project: Change the World."*

I am writing, most importantly, to ask for your prayer support. (This is the universal sentence of every support-request letter we have ever read from any kid—including our own.) *I would also like to ask for your financial support.* (Of course, this sentence is also universal!) *I need to raise a minimum of $500* (or $1,000 or $1,500) *in order to be a part of this ministry team. I would appreciate your response as soon as possible, but if you cannot give, I will certainly understand.*

Thank you for considering me and "Project: Change the World" in your prayers.

Your friend,

Mark

(And again that personal touch, a handwritten signature.)

But after the initial reading, and sorting through the twenty or so young Marks we know (trying to figure out what this one's last name is), we remember the impact such opportunities had on our own sons. We would hate for any kid we know to miss the spiritually formative opportunities the church holds. We would even hate for any kid we *don't* know to miss these opportunities! And so we drop a check into the return envelope and by so doing we are *not* saying to Mark Whatever-his-name-is, "Take a hike!" No. We are saying, "Catch a ride, kid. Go with the winds of the Spirit. Try your wings. We hope Tunisia survives you!"

In so many ways the opportunities available to kids in the church say, "Try your wings."

Yes, the church is often the place that endures (and, amazingly, still manages to encourage) our first musical solos, our first public speeches, our first attempts to lead or teach or organize. You've been there. You know what we mean. You've sat in the congregation and listened to entire songs sung in the wrong octave or the wrong key by a novice Amy Grant wanna-be. Painful. You've managed not to wince at trumpets that blare and clarinets that squeak. You've said a prayer while some child shivers with fear as he or she speaks. You've held your tongue while some leader-in-training tries to organize a youth-sponsored car wash or fund-raising supper that is doomed, doomed, doomed.

Like us, you may (for a brief moment) roll your eyes when the requests for support come; but like us, you probably give.

Why do you and I support these things?

Because we know how important it is for kids to become all God made them to be. We know that the support of the church family may make all the difference in children's discovering their spiritual gifts, their potential, and in learning that there is a place in the kingdom only they can fill. We know a kid's gotta fly if life is going to be sweet. Walking isn't enough. Crawling through life could shrivel their spirits and break their hearts. Life has to have a purpose, a meaning, a reason for breathing air and taking up space.

The church can help our children find out why they are here and what they are meant to do—to discover a sense of mission, a cause worth giving their lives for. The hearts of God's people are amazingly absorbent. Like a spiritual shock absorber they sustain the false starts, painful beginnings, and shaky middles of most of our lives.

There is just nothing like the church!

CHURCH: A PLACE THAT NEEDS US

But sometimes the church isn't so great. We all know that. We can be disappointed when it falls short of its best potential. It seems even unchurched people have a pretty good idea of what church should be like. When it's political or uncaring or spiritually tepid, it can be so disappointing.

It's at those times parents might be tempted to give their kids a pass, to become less involved, or to become critical about the church themselves.

But it's exactly when church seems a bitter pill that parents need their own speeches. "If it's not good, then you go and make it better. Be a healer where there's disease. Be a leader where there's no direction. Make a difference in your own piece of the kingdom."

We all need the church. It is formative in our own lives. And we need other believers in the wider community of faith to fill in the gaps, to offer belonging and celebration and encouragement to our kids.

The church needs us as well. And the church needs you. To be everything she can be—a city on a hill, salt and light, we all need to shine and season and illuminate this dark and lost world.

May all our children be captured by a passion for the church. Even when it falls short, or misses the mark, or blows it now and then, there's still nothing like the church. You've gotta love it!

NOTE

1. Refer to Resource Article 2, beginning on page 169, for a user friendly tool called "The Sunday Search." It can help parents build into your family the value of encountering God at church.

For the LORD *is good and his love endures forever;*
his faithfulness continues through all generations.
. . . .

—PSALM 100:5

Lesson Nine

YOUR FAMILY
IS A LIVING LINK
IN A CHAIN OF FAITH

Valerie embarrassed two twelve-year-old twin brothers recently. She knew her action was over the edge, but says she couldn't help herself! Right. As soon as she saw the two boys she was instantly drawn to them, which in her mind gave enough license for eccentric behavior.

We were visiting our former church in South Florida where I had been a youth pastor right out of graduate school. All of those "youth groups" are middle-aged adults now with teenagers of their own. But whenever we reconnect with any of them, when we meet their children (mostly strangers to us), we have an amazing sense of linkage to their families that time and distance can never diminish. I find Valerie's version of what happened authentic and innocent:

"When I was introduced to these twin boys I was overwhelmed with an immediate sense of affection for them—because I had adored their mother when she was about the same age. I could see in them her eyes and hair, her way of deporting herself. I just grabbed them, hugged them, planted quick kisses on their foreheads, enjoyed their embarrassment and said, 'You don't know me, but I love your mother!'"

At that age, it's embarrassing enough to have a mother. You really shouldn't have to deal with her strange friends on top of it!

Valerie and I have noticed through the years that the children of the friends we love always maintain a special place in our hearts. We just love them because we love their parents. And so, it seems, it is with God.

God has a perspective on our lives unbound by time. He sees us as we stand at the present, but He also sees us as a link in a generational chain, the child or grandchild or great-great-grandchild (or all of the above) of a precious friend of His. He doesn't only love us for us. He also is a friend to someone to whom we matter.

A CHAIN OF SPIRITUAL HERITAGE

As younger parents, we had a pretty narrow view of family. Part of our spiritual journey included broadening this perspective to become more aware that God's faithfulness wasn't just about "us four and no more." We belonged to a chain of spiritual heritage. We were experiencing blessing because of our parents and grandparents and great-grandparents who had been friends with God.

Let us open this perspective for you. The members of our families who have been God's friends go back many centuries. For instance, we know that our children belong to a faith chain that goes back at least to the seventeenth century. Valerie's ancestors were Huguenots back then—French Protestants—persecuted, stripped of possessions and rights, and driven from France to Holland. Abraham LaRue, living in exile in Holland, married there and had two sons and a daughter.

But even then, life was far from good. Desperate for a new life, Abraham sold himself to an English sea captain as an indentured servant to pay for passage to America for himself, his wife, and three children. The plan was that when they reached America the sea captain would sell Abraham to a landowner, to whom he would be under contract for the next four to seven years.

That was the plan, but then the unthinkable happened. Abraham died on shipboard and was buried at sea. The captain would have his payment in flesh, however. To pay for the voyage, the English sea captain put Abraham's three children in chains and attempted to sell them when they reached Rhode Island. The mother was freed but heartbroken.

What desperate prayers that widowed mother must have lain at God's heart! She also got up off her knees, refusing to accept such a fate for her children. Instead, she stole back onto the ship and with a handspike managed to break open the chains and rescue her two sons. Sadly, she was unable to free her daughter.

We admire this courageous Christian woman even from the distance of several centuries. Valerie and our children are links in her family chain, clasped through the centuries through faith and DNA.

In a later century, we are linked to a woman in Kentucky, who was a "granny" woman, a midwife. She is said to have been a woman of great beauty, as well as unusual intellectual accomplishments. She studied medicine, even though her second husband opposed this interest and confined her to what he considered "the woman's sphere." But she was not prevented from answering a call on February 12, 1809, from a tenant farmer by the name of Thomas Lincoln to deliver a baby boy to his wife, Nancy Hanks Lincoln. Abraham Lincoln began life under the tender care of this woman of faith and accomplishment.

We take comfort from knowing that our sons belong to such a line of faith and friendship with God. We love to tell these stories to our boys. Family faith stories are so powerful, convey such belonging, and provide such a stable grounding for children's spiritual lives that we need to cherish them. When we experience the benefits of family stories, we wonder why parents don't tap into family faith histories more often.

Spiritual histories have a powerful impact on the faith formation of children. As children ourselves, hearing the adults in our families talk about our faith ancestry, both of us can remember those heartfelt strong connections in our own growing up years. These accounts were like links of belonging and anchors of grounding. Today, as adults, we understand that our lives are experiencing the "trickle down" blessing of generations on both sides of our families—Bells and Burtons—that have been, throughout time, friends with God.

A BREAK IN THE CHAIN OF FAITH

Sometimes, life is not so sweet. At such times, when our children give us cause to worry and reason to pray, when the "fig tree does not bud and there are no grapes on the vines, though the olive crop fails and the fields produce no food, though there are no sheep in the pen and no cattle in the stalls" (Habakkuk 3:17), then our family stories comfort us.

We remember another link in this family chain. His children gave him cause for concern. Very often when I (Valerie) sit on a plane going to some speaking engagement, I muse about this man. He was my great-grandfather, Charles LaRue, a Methodist circuit preacher in Oklahoma. During the week he farmed cotton, but each weekend he traveled to a different congregation to preach, marry, and baptize. I am an apple that did not fall far from that particular tree. We share the same calling, traveling in order to speak about Jesus, Charles on horseback, me in "the friendly skies."

But at one point, this godly man feared he had suffered a break in the long chain of faith. In those days, public entertainment often meant gathering in parlors, churches, town squares, or halls to debate and discuss the issues of the day—politics, religion, community issues, and philosophy. Verbal skills were admired and enjoyed by all. And the family oral history recounts that there were two particularly skilled verbal men in Clinton, Oklahoma, in those days. One was my great-grandfather, the preacher Charles LaRue, descendent of Huguenots, defender of the faith and friend of God.

The other was Greenberry Burton (yes, his real name), farmer, nonchurchgoer, illiterate but street smart, possessed with a wicked, self-deprecating humor that refused to take himself, or anyone else, including preacher men, too seriously. He could be charmingly ornery. He was my *other* great-grandfather.

When Charles said black, Greenberry said white. When Charles lectured, "Thus saith the Lord!" Greenberry rolled his eyes and chuckled back a "Who says so?" They were polar opposites.

And when Charles's daughter, Rosa, fell in love and married Greenberry's son, William Mack Burton, it broke her preacher-father's heart. He felt that a man of seemingly private faith was actually a man of no real faith . . . certainly not his own evangelical brand to be sure. He grieved to think that the most precious of all links in his life, the one that included his daughter and future grandchildren, had embraced (in his opinion) one of the worst heritages the little town of Clinton, Oklahoma, had to offer.

GOD SEES THE ETERNAL PICTURE

Charles could not see the bigger, more inclusive picture. It was as if the man lived in a vacuum while God lives in eternity. God looked at Charles and saw beyond what was currently happening. God recalled a desperate widowed mother with a spike in her hands and a daughter left in chains. He had comforted her with a promised blessing even while her life crumbled around her. It was undoubtedly a blessing in promise, one she might not fully experience during her own lifetime, but one that would be known by her children and her grandchildren. This blessing has been trickling down for generations.

God's perspective on Charles's heartbreak also included a beautiful woman struggling to be all God made her to be. And even while her husband held her back, God blessed her with honor—to be the tender hands and wise heart that delivered a baby of great promise and blessing—Abraham Lincoln—to a world that would desperately need him in a few short years.

God also saw into the centuries to come—to my parents' generation and beyond, including our own children's children. "For now we see through a glass, darkly . . ." (1 Corinthians 13:12 KJV), but He knows what the bigger picture holds for the future in this family chain of faith.

God saw Charles as a living link in that long chain of faith. And because Charles was a friend of God's, we can understand that Charles's children and grandchildren mattered to Him. But God is incredibly big-hearted. Greenberry mattered to Him as well, as did his children and grandchildren. And so even while Charles mourned, God was planning to strengthen the family chain. From the benefit of several succeeding generations, we know now what Charles did not know during his own lifetime. And it is this—that even to the second, third, and fourth generations, God has been his family's friend. The chain of faith continues.

During these men's lifetimes, an amazing set of events began to unfold. Greenberry's wife became a Christ follower, as did each of their children. While he was still living, one of his sons even went into the ministry. I remember his son Mack, my grandfather, to be a godly and humble churchman. And though his wife, Rosa, died as a young woman during childbirth, her letters are full of the sweetness indicative of a woman of faith.

Amazingly, the generations that followed do not seem traceable to or influenced by Greenberry but, rather, to have been marked by a strong leaning toward lay and professional ministry. God is writing this family's annals—no one else!

Recently a branch of the descendants of the LaRue/Burton family gathered in California. Steve and I were able to make the trip, and we all attended church together, sitting side by side, filling a number of pews. As our voices melded in a hymn of praise that morning, I couldn't help but think of all our family members descended from Charles. God's faithfulness to all the generations of this man's family has been so good.

In heaven on that particular Sunday morning, I wondered if perhaps Charles sang along with his own song of praise to the God who was and is and will continue to be his family Friend!

WOUNDING TO BLESS

It's natural to grieve when a child turns away from faith. But it is also important to continue to trust—believing that, even though it may look bleak at the moment, God will not overlook your friendship or the child who matters to you.[1] God's faithfulness is still being poured out on the generations of Charles LaRue—friend of God.

That can be God's outcome for your family as well. God has good intentions for you and your family. His desire, sometimes through much pain and many wounds, is to bless those who turn to Him, in spite of their history or circumstances.

Scripture gives us a look at the heart of God in this matter. Jacob came from a family line of faith. His grandfather, Abraham, walked with God and had received a blessing in promise about the future generations of his family. Jacob's father, Isaac, was also a man of faith. But Jacob was the weak link in the family faith chain. He was untrustworthy, capable of betraying his family through stealing and manipulation. He was the family black sheep, a real rascal!

But when God saw Jacob, He also had the long picture in view. He had not forgotten His friends Abraham and Isaac. He remembered the past, but He also looked into the future. In His knowledge of eternity, God recognized Jacob's importance to the redemption story. God was concerned about Jacob because Jacob was in the "line of promise."[2] This line of promise had begun with Abraham long before when God honored Abraham's friendship with the promise that he would be the father of a great nation. Fulfilling God's vow to Abraham meant that this weak link, Jacob, would need to be strengthened. What an extent God went to in order to bring this rascal into line.

Let's pick up Jacob's story in Genesis 32 at a crucial point. After years of scheming and finally burning all his relational bridges with Laban—his equally crafty father-in-law—Jacob, as a last resort, turned back to his own family. But he feared Esau, his twin brother, whom he had cheated out of his birthright years before. On Jacob's anxious journey back home, the Scriptures tell us "the angels of God met him" (Genesis 32:1). It must have been quite a sight, because Jacob called these angelic messengers "God's army!" (verse 2 AMP).

Apparently even an army did not suffice to turn the prodigal around. A stronger impression needed to be made on him. That night, while Jacob was alone, a man appeared to him. They wrestled all through the night. Toward morning, when the man saw that He couldn't overpower Jacob, He wounded him with a supernatural kind of maiming. "He touched the socket of Jacob's hip so that his hip was wrenched as he wrestled" (verse 25). Jacob recognized that this battle scar was of God. Finally grasping that his combatant was not human but a heavenly visitor, he grabbed Him and would not let Him go until this "superhuman" had blessed him.

This was the blessing: "Your name will no longer be Jacob, but Israel, because you have struggled with God and with men and have overcome" (verse 28).

This supernatural visitor's prophecy came true. The very next day, instead of receiving the hostility he deserved from his twin brother, Esau, he was welcomed home. His name was changed from Jacob to Israel. To what a great extent—both wounding and blessing—God went, in order to preserve Abraham and Isaac's blessing and family chain of faith.

GOD'S HEART TOWARD PARENTS AND CHILDREN

Parents of "rascals" can take comfort from God's dealings with Jacob. The shape of a child's soul, his or her receptivity to God, is a special concern of every parent who loves God. Maybe as you're reading this book you're grasping for some special insight in how God works in the soul of a child, especially a child who couldn't care less. Or perhaps you're at the end of your rope. You have done everything you know to do. You have read the books, attended the seminars. Your life, your prayers, your priorities have all been adjusted in order to woo your child to Christ. But through almost unbearable heartache you have watched your child shape to everything but faith.

To watch a child pursue a dissolute life, to love a child who shapes his or her soul to drugs or alcohol, sexual promiscuity, immorality, and lawlessness, or just everyday disbelief is a special agony for a believing parent. We understand. That's why before we bring this book to conclusion we want to highlight a special perspective that may provide some needed hope.

We want to encourage you to remember God's heart toward your child. Through the years we have observed four important characteristics of God's heart toward parents and children. Whether you parent a rascal or not, allow these observations to build your faith.

GOD IS TRUSTWORTHY

First, God honors your friendship. That means you can trust God to go to amazing extents to bring your child to faith. Yes, it's true, that theologically speaking God has no grandchildren—every person must come to a personal decision to place his or her faith in Jesus Christ as Savior, as an individual act of response to God. Your child can reject faith. That's all true.

But it's also not the whole story!

God is a relational God, and He is "not wanting anyone to perish" (2 Peter 3:9). "God so loved the world . . . ," which means the children of His friends matter to Him. And though God has no grandchildren, it's also true that if you are His friend, then God is also your family friend. This means that every child, including the child of a faith-filled parent, is "on God's screen." When parents are puzzled, God knows the answers. When parents worry, God is confident. When parents are powerless, God is powerful. Mostly, God's ways with our children are delightful and gentle. But if it is necessary, as it was with Jacob, God may wound in order to bless.

God may go to amazing lengths with your child to honor His friendship with you. This could even include wounding a child in order to bless that child. The following Old Testament passage records a sampling of God's extensive "return to me" methods:

> "I sent you hunger," says the Lord, "but it did no good; you still would not return to me. I ruined your crops by holding back the rain. . . . there wasn't ever enough [to drink]. Yet you wouldn't return to me," says the Lord.
>
> "I sent blight and mildew on your farms and vineyards; the locusts ate your figs and olive trees. And still you wouldn't return to me," says the Lord. "I sent you plagues like those of Egypt long ago. I killed your lads in war and drove away your horses. The stench of death was terrible to smell. And yet you refused to come. I destroyed some of your cities. . . . And still you won't return to me," says the Lord.
>
> "Therefore I will bring upon you . . . further evils. . . . For you are dealing with the one who formed the mountains and made the winds, and knows your every thought . . . : Jehovah, the Lord, the God of Hosts, is his name." (Amos 4:6–13 TLB)

God is not without options when it comes to getting the attention of a weak link in the family chain. Make no doubt about it, sometimes God will wound those He loves to get our attention, to help us return to Him, to get us to the place where He can bless us.

A PARENT'S RESPONSE TO
GOD'S "WOUNDING TO BLESS"

How should a parent take this? We are not suggesting that parents take any pleasure in the "wounding to bless" ways of God. "Well, kid, you're just going to have to suffer the consequences" should always be spoken with a tender heart toward a wayward son or daughter. We are simply reminding you that you are not in this struggle alone. God cares for you, and what matters to you matters to God. He may use His superhuman resources to restore the broken link. In your lifetime, or in your generation, you may not get to see the whole picture. In time and in His ways, God will bless your family. In eternity, prodigals do not have the final word, nor do they write the final chapter.

GOD IS AT WORK . . . ALWAYS

Second, God will not give up. When life looks bleak, at least from a parent's perspective, God continues to work. There is no such thing as "too far gone" with God. A mother of a recently returned prodigal described to us the nightmare of her son's life without God. Drugs and alcohol addictions, arrests, trials, sentencings, an illegitimate baby, violent behavior, and unemployment marked his years after high school. His twenties—the "get-yourself-established" decade—was wasted and totally swallowed up, defined primarily by abusing drugs and alcohol. Lance (not his real name) was unemployable, unmarriageable, and unrepentant.

Then two years ago his life sustained a wound that blessed him. A judge, in a desperate act of intervention, sentenced him to a lengthy stay at a Christian drug and alcohol rehabilitation center. Lance was no longer free, no longer treated as a responsible adult, and no longer left to make his own decisions.

It was exactly what he needed. With intense effort and intentionality he let God turn his life around. Recently, Lance reflected with his mom about his lowest points. "Even on my trips to buy drugs, while I was in the car on my way, I prayed—I prayed for release. I prayed for willpower to turn my life around. I prayed for intervention. I prayed for God to send me a miracle."

What does this mean? It means that although his life was destructively on the skids, Lance was never completely given over to the darkness. He could see the difference between himself and his other drug-addicted friends. "They weren't like me, Mom. I mean we were all messed up, including me, but they didn't struggle. They just abandoned themselves to their own destruction. They didn't pray for strength to turn. There was very little agonizing over the consequences of their choices. They only cared about getting high, their next 'fix.' That's all. Nothing else. They seemed without conscience, to be totally given over to their depravity."

What an amazing insight. Most people sizing up his life at that point would have written *him* off—thought he'd blown it for good. What they couldn't have known was that this young man always had a small ray of light shining into the darkest places of his soul. No one knew it was there except for him. And he could only admit it *after* his life turned around!

We think Lance's words are hopeful for parents who are worried about their kids. Regardless of how bad it looks, there is a good possibility that your child has only one foot in the wrong place. The other foot may still be straddling the fence. Down deep that child's heart may be *longing* for a better life, even if at the moment it appears to be beating only for the wrong things. There is a good possibility that his or her soul has not totally shaped to the darkness. God shines in incredibly dark places and will not abandon your child.

That means we should never stop praying, even when the situation seems most bleak or hopeless. It's essential to pray persistently that God will get through to a son or daughter who seemingly could not care less about spiritual life—even if God must wound in order to bless. Some parents make a strategic mistake in overly protecting kids from the consequences of their choices. Trusting God may sometimes mean staying out of the way so that He can get a kid's attention.

It's also important as we pray for such a child that we pray that Satan will be bound, that no harm outside of God's care will wound this child, and that no amount of damage that may occur will break up the family. Satan wounds to destroy; God wounds to bless. And we must pray for the wisdom to discern the difference.

Here's an enormously important point we want to emphasize as well. Just as you are unyielding in prayer, be as equally relentless in throwing out the "hope" lifeline, even if you have a hard time believing it yourself.

"You are never too far gone for God to love you, for God to help you, for God to restore and redeem your life. You have a future and a hope. You are precious to Him."

Many people, including children, can often think themselves "too far gone" for God to reach. They constantly hear the hopeless voice of accusation and damnation. If you love such a one, one of the best services you could offer is to help him or her hear God's voice of hope. Keep that lifeline ready and near the water so a hand can grab it some desperate day.

THE GOD OF NEW BEGINNINGS

Third, the God of the Bible is the God of new beginnings. What if you don't have a record of family faith? Maybe your story is exactly the opposite; you're the first believer in perhaps a long lineage of rascals. Then you may be unaware of your spiritual history, or any family stories of faith. But God has begun a new work in you. Your story of coming to faith is the place to begin. If you are the first believer in a family of nonbelievers, then God is your friend. God cares about what matters to you. And what matters most to you is your family, your children. We all have to start somewhere. Tell your faith story to your kids. Show them how God worked on you, called you, redeemed you, and changed you. Awe them with the family annals that begin with you.

THE FINAL CHAPTER HAS NOT BEEN WRITTEN

Finally, never forget that God writes the final chapter. Valerie and I have learned to look at life through a different set of lenses since we began to write books together a number of years ago. In the middle of some of the biggest messes, the most intense stresses, and incredibly frustrating circumstances, a part of us doesn't experience it at all. That part is registering the experience, but instead of thinking, *This is just awful . . . how is this going to turn out?* the writer part is thinking, *This is book material, what a great illustration, just what's needed—for someday. Terrific!*

Actually, everybody's life is book material. All of us are like chapters in God's many generational story of man's redemption. So when a child you love begins to "write his life" in disastrous themes, you can be comforted to know that this falling away is just a chapter, not the entire book. This particular heartbreak is more than heartbreak; it's part of a great unfolding story that will someday be told, but only after God has the final word and adds the final period. Which He most definitely will.

We leave you with that comfort.

A PRAYER OF BLESSING

We also leave you with this blessing for you and the children you love:

May your children be Christ followers, shaped and molded to the heart of God.

May they be gifted in faith, overachievers in trusting God.

When they are babies, may their peanut butter prayers build a fortress of spiritual power that stuns into impotence all evil that might try to take them.

Through their growing up years, may your home's hallways be filled with angels and the rhythm of your souls accompanied by angel choirs.

May you travel together through the most dangerous places life might take you, confident in God—sure and without wobble in your faith.

May your child have an early bent and openness to God that emerges into a significant role to fill in God's kingdom to come.

May you and your child discover the warmth and acceptance—the belonging, the joy of celebration, the renewed perspective on what really matters, and the safe and stimulating place for enriching your spiritual walk with Christ—that can only be experienced in God's wider community, the church.

In your family chain of faith, may your children be the strongest links—the ones the stories will be told about for generations to come.

And specifically for you, Mom or Dad, may your own soul grow to a greater capacity for faith because you parent the soul of a child.

May you walk closer to God and follow Christ more devotedly.

May your sensitivity to the things of the Spirit become heightened.

May you become more skilled at recognizing the ways of God in the soul of man.

And when your children remember you, may they always realize how very blessed they are to have had such a parent of great and enduring faith.

May the blessings of your friendship with God trickle down for generations to come.

Amen and amen.

NOTES

1. If you're coping with a wayward son or daughter, read Resource Article 4, "Going the Distance with Your Prodigal Child," for further information and encouragement.
2. Billy Graham, *Angels: God's Secret Agents* (Waco. Tex.: Word, 1994), 86.

. . . .

FAMILY
RESOURCE
ARTICLES

. . . .

Family Resource Article 1

THE GOD HUNT

BECOMING AN EXPERT AT
FINDING GOD IN THE EVERYDAY

B ack in 1987, when our boys were still quite young, the head-
line on a magazine cover caught my attention, and I couldn't
put it down until I had read it through completely. "Fourteen Great Minds Predict the Future." That was the title—and that's
all it took to hook me!

The article began, "Looking into the future is often a little like
charting unexplored territory; it creates great exhilaration and immense
uncertainty."[1] The article's focus was what the next twenty years will
likely bring in the major fields of human endeavor—including the
sciences, economics, politics, the arts, education, plus the field
Valerie and I have spent a major chunk of our lives in—communi-
cations. The experts included Bill Gates of Microsoft Corporation

and Tony Verna of Global Media (who also was the inventor of TV's instant replay).

"The processing of digital (or computerized) information is improving very quickly," Gates declared. "In ten years you'll have thirty to forty times as much computational power [which obviously has already come to pass!] and you'll be able to manipulate the images and sounds that you now receive just passively from TV—you'll be able to insert yourself into a game or [get this!] you can even change the outcome according to your wishes."

Verna predicted that in twenty years, instead of TV, the images you'll watch will be projected by lasers. The images will appear in our living rooms (or wherever we want) without a screen, wherever the laser beams converge—kind of a theater in the round. Sounded unbelievable back in 1987, but it doesn't seem so far-fetched these days.

But add to that this new angle he included almost fifteen years ago as he predicted things to come: "sensavision." No longer will you be just watching those images, but through the use of a headset, something like a Walkman (but attached to your forehead) you'll actually be able to *feel* what's happening. For example, by the year 2007 you'll be able to watch a live concert on stage from any place in the world, and when the performer feels hot and sweaty, you'll feel the heat. Or if a spray of water splashes an athlete in the face, you'll feel that. However, according to this expert, sensavision will probably require some kind of computer cut-off point to prevent the emotional sensations from getting too intense—especially, if you're watching a car race when the race-car driver crashes!

Another expert, Timothy Leary, president of Futique Software Company, suggested that in 2007 you'll be living in an information society in which information will be what money and machinery were in the Industrial Age. According to this man, everyone is going to be a psychologist, a computer whiz, and a philosopher. Mind play, mind performance, and psychological skills are going to be the equivalent of land, money, and power in the earlier ages.

Leary also predicted that in twenty years everyone is going to be responsible for government. It'll be done by televoting—perhaps every Sunday between noon and 1:00 o'clock. And furthermore he presumed with the ability to vote directly through personal computers, there won't be any more need for representation. So according to this expert, politicians will become obsolete. Now wouldn't that be something!

This same expert predicted that in the first decade of the twenty-first century drugs will be old-fashioned. Because by then there'll be special transmitters available that will pick up and communicate with the electricity in your brain—a kind of brain radio that will fit in your ear like a hearing aid. So instead of using drugs or chemicals, with a turn of a dial you can tune into any emotional, mental, or sensual experience you want. The key to the twenty-first century, says this man, will be five words: "Think for yourself; question authority."

Sounds frightening, doesn't it?

The predictions went on and on: Football players tackled in our own living rooms; toss-away disposable computers; life in ten dimensions—I don't even know what that means!

Admittedly some of these things sound fascinating. But whether they'll come to pass by the year 2007, just a few years from now, who can say? And whether our lives will be better or worse, or more stress-filled, because of these advances—who really knows?

A PREDICTION YOU CAN COUNT ON

However, there is one prediction that I can make with absolute certainty that pertains to the *near* future. And it has the potential to make everyone's life immeasurably better. In fact, what I'm going to suggest is a skill anyone can develop that's basic to helping each of us learn how to manage all of life—including family life—and survive the increasingly fast-pace and multiple distractions of this new millennium. And best of all I'm talking about something that could take place in a relatively short time—within the next few months even! Now that's a far cry from a twenty year prediction; but, right now, likely most of us Dads and Moms are more concerned about getting through the next couple of months than we are the next two decades!

Here's my prediction: *When you recognize the reality of Christ's supernatural presence in your life and home, you will live on the edge of expectancy.*

163

Now I'm talking about that spiritual dimension that even some Christian people say: "I don't even know what that means!" Oh, they want to see the image of Christ before them, but they just can't seem to get the natural and supernatural laser beams to converge.

GOD WITHIN OUR REACH

I doubt that any of us who are Christ followers has a problem accepting this theological truth: *Christ is with us.* This is a basic tenet of the Christian faith that most believers hold on to fiercely. Where some do struggle, though, is knowing this experientially—in the everyday. Here's a user-friendly family resource, a simple tool that has had a huge impact on our immediate family during the past twenty years. Putting this tool to work in your home could begin to help you and your family discover the reality of Christ's supernatural presence in your everyday lives. It can contribute to having faith-shaped kids.

Think with me for a moment—this is an incredible truth: If you're a Christian believer—a person of faith—then Jesus Christ, the God-man, the Creator of the universe, by His Spirit is living in your life right now. That's more exciting than anything predicted in the article from the fourteen experts! And the beautiful thing is, not one of us has to wait for a number of years to pass in order for sensavision to be perfected to experience His presence. No!

Each of us can, today, know personally the reality and involvement of Christ in our life. You simply need to sharpen your spiritual focus and, with your eyes of faith, find the God who is already there.

The reality is God *wants* to be involved in our lives. According to Paul in the book of Acts, "The God who made the world and everything in it . . . gives all men life and breath and everything else. . . . [This same God desires] . . . that men would seek him and perhaps reach out for him and find him" (17:24–27). Then Paul adds, "He is not far from each one of us."

I'm sure all of us understand this in a textbook kind of way, but on a daily functional level—the way we live—some of us are more like the disciple Thomas. Thomas was also a kind of expert—he was an expert at doubting.

Following the resurrection of Jesus, "when the other disciples told

Thomas that they had seen the Lord, he declared, 'Unless I see [physical evidence like] the nail marks in his hands and put my finger where the nails were, and put my hand into his side, I will not believe it.'"

One week later Jesus appeared to all the disciples. "Though the doors were locked, Jesus came and stood among them, and said, 'Peace be with you!' Then he said to Thomas, 'Put your finger here; see my hands. Reach out your hand and put it into my side'" (John 20:25–27).

How's that for first century "sensavision"?

And then Jesus said, "Stop doubting and believe."

Perhaps these are the same words Christ is saying to some of us right now. "Stop doubting and believe." In other words: "I want to be involved in your life!" When you recognize the reality of Christ's supernatural presence in your life and home, you will live on the edge of expectancy.

I suspect Jesus has worked on your and my behalf many times in the past and for whatever reason, we didn't notice. You know, those times He's answered our prayers—even the little ones—and then the lost keys suddenly reappeared or the missing book, file folder, wristwatch, article of clothing, whatever . . . was found. How about occasions when He's helped you accomplish a task you didn't think you had the energy, or maybe even the ability, to do? Or have you ever received some unexpected funds just in time to pay a pressing bill?

Coincidence? Maybe you thought so at the time, but Valerie and I and our family choose to believe that these happenings are touches of the supernatural—Christ saying: "I'm here . . . Stop doubting and believe. Acknowledge *My* involvement! Go ahead and give the credit to Me."

BASIC INGREDIENTS TO THE GOD HUNT

Recognizing such happenings is to discover what we call "God Hunt sightings." Such sightings will build your faith and that of your children. This family exercise known as The God Hunt originated with Valerie's sister and brother-in-law, Karen and David Mains, who cohosted the national radio broadcast *The Chapel of the Air* since the late 1970s. David and Karen originated this concept and, by the time we arrived on the scene in the early 1980s to assist with the broadcast, they had already been going on a daily God Hunt with their four children for a number of years.

How do you make a God Hunt sighting? Such sightings typically consist of one of four events:

1. any obvious answer to prayer;
2. special help to accomplish ministry tasks;
3. unexpected evidence of God's care; or
4. an unusual linkage or timing.

Whatever might fit one of these categories can be viewed as merely coincidence or . . . we can *choose*—as we're suggesting we should all learn to do—to give the credit to Christ.

"YOUR ASSIGNMENT, SHOULD YOU CHOOSE TO ACCEPT IT"

You and your family (but beginning with you first) *can* become adept at giving Christ the credit—not just mentally or passively but by keeping track of these sightings. Whenever Christ startles you as He did His disciple Thomas—by suddenly giving evidence of His presence—make note of it. In fact, we suggest that you go so far as to keep a record of the specific times Christ acts on your behalf by jotting these things down on a sheet of paper or in a daily diary or calendar. Better yet, create a family God Hunt journal or notebook to keep track of these supernatural encounters.

Valerie and I have been doing The God Hunt exercise for nearly twenty years now, and over the long haul we have discovered it's a practical and delightful way to engage our children naturally in everyday spiritual conversation. Going on a daily God Hunt will help your family to discover together God's activity in your lives. Also, creating and keeping up with an official record of God's involvement with each family member will add a vitality and healthy dynamic to any home on which you can build for years to come.

In the classic work *The Pursuit of God*, A.W. Tozer wrote, "The impulse to pursue God originates with God, but the outworking of that impulse is our following hard after Him, and all the time we are pursuing Him we are already in His hand: 'Thy right hand uphold-eth me.' In this divine 'upholding' and human 'following' there is no contradiction. All is of God, for as von Hugel teaches, *God is always previous.* In practice, however, . . . man must pursue God."[2]

It's on this principle that The God Hunt is based. Hunting, or pur-suing after God, is a specific lifetime skill that believers need to de-velop every day. It's a never-ending process, an ongoing search for both young and old. And when shared together it can become an increasing joy and family glue that, based upon our experience, will never grow old. Becoming an expert at discovering God's activity in your life and home is, bottom line, the art of learning to recog-nize God's hand and touch on your daily world.

When you recognize the reality of Christ's supernatural pres-ence in your life and home, you will live on the edge of expectancy. Why? Because you never know for sure what's going to happen next! But you always know that something of spiritual significance is go-ing to take place, because God is always at work in your life, my life, and the lives of our children.

ENCOURAGEMENT FOR SKEPTICS

In case you're worried about not being able to find God at work in your life, take confidence in these words of Scripture:

- Moses: "If . . . you seek the Lord your God, you will find him if you look for Him with all your heart and with all your soul" (Deuteronomy 4:29).
- David, publicly addressing Solomon, just before Solomon suc-ceeds him as King of Israel: "My son Solomon . . . serve [God] with wholehearted devotion and with a willing mind . . . If you seek him, he will be found by you" (1 Chronicles 28:9).
- Isaiah: "Seek the Lord while he may be found; call on him while he is near" (Isaiah 55:6).
- The Lord Himself declares: "You will seek me and find me when you seek me with all your heart. I will be found by you" (Jere-miah 29:13–14).

• And from the lips of Jesus:"Seek and you will find ... For everyone ... who seeks finds" (Matthew 7:7–8).

This is but a small sampling of the scores of verses throughout the Old and New Testaments that verify this basic concept: "If you look for God, you'll find Him, and you'll experience the joy of discovery!"

Stop doubting and believe. When you recognize the reality of Christ's supernatural presence in your life, you will live on the edge of expectancy. Why marvel about what the experts say is going to happen in the years ahead when *right now* you can experience the miracle presence of Christ in your own life!

DON'T MISS THIS

One final prediction: If you genuinely look for Christ's active involvement in your own life—you *will* find Him. Promise.

And, if you start a family God Hunt notebook and stay at it, after a few months, years, and decades, as you "Tell it to your children, and let your children tell it to their children, and their children to the next generation" (Joel 1:3)—in this matter of recognizing God in the everyday—you'll become an expert yourself, and people will want to hear what *you* have to say!

NOTES

1. Marion Long, "Fourteen Great Minds Predict the Future." *Omni,* January, 1987, 38.
2. A. W. Tozer, *The Pursuit of God* (Camp Hill, Pa.: Christian Publications, 1982), 12.

THE SUNDAY SEARCH

A FAMILY GUIDE TO BETTER CHURCH EXPERIENCES

I couldn't help overhearing their conversation as we walked out of the church service. The two men were only a couple of steps in front of me when the younger one asked, "Well, what did you think?"

The other man, probably in his mid-forties, responded without hesitation and began what turned out to be a rather lengthy description of everything he *didn't like* about the pastor's sermon.

Exactly how long this negative monologue lasted, I don't know. But Valerie and I got in on at least three or four minutes' worth—all the way to the church parking lot.

I wasn't eavesdropping intentionally, but what they were saying caught my ear, and then I couldn't keep myself from listening to every word. The critical tone of the conversation really bothered me. In fact, the more I thought about it, the more heartsick I became. You see, for me the worship service had been very meaningful.

I had especially appreciated the sermon that morning because the Lord used something the pastor had said to speak directly to me. I needed to hear the point that was made, and it came through as if the Lord Himself had said it. His presence had been so real to me! I was leaving church refreshed and upbeat—until I happened upon the conversation just described.

SPONTANEOUS OBSERVATIONS

What if someone had approached *you* right after last weekend's church service with that same question, "Well, what did you think?" What might *you* have said? Now, I'm talking about someone with whom you could be completely honest—no need to put on any airs or cushion your words. What spontaneous observations would you have made?

Perhaps your comments would be critical too: "Well, the service was dull, and the preacher went on too long again!" Or, "The choir sure leaves a lot to be desired. There are a couple of people in that soprano section who ought to be replaced."

Or maybe your response would have been more positive but not necessarily for the right reasons: "The pastor's sermon was great today—he really kept my attention with all those funny stories he told …and (miracle of miracles!) we actually got out on time for a change!"

It's occurred to both Valerie and me over the years that, typically, most Christians don't ask the right questions when evaluating their worship experience. Perhaps it's also fair to say that most Christians don't consciously evaluate their worship experience at all! And those who do usually come to their conclusions without considering the proper criteria.

I guess this shouldn't be startling. Most people, including you and me, have been significantly influenced by our "have it your way" society. When evaluating anything, the typical mind-set gravitates to questions like:

"How did it please me?"

"Did I like it?"

"Do I deserve better?"

So, transferring this kind of thinking to what happens in church, it's no wonder that we tend to focus on peripheral issues like the length of the service, the performance level of the musicians, or whether or not the sermon was entertaining.

I don't want to imply that these matters are of no consequence. I think it's understood that most of us endorse and want to work hard toward achieving quality and excellence in all areas, especially when it comes to matters of faith. But when evaluating your church experience (and I think it's something we should all do every weekend!), it's important to consider the issues that really matter. In the building-up-our-faith-department it's going to be a decided advantage for any of us as we learn to address ourselves to questions that are truly *spiritually* significant.

LEARNING TO ASK THE RIGHT QUESTIONS

That's why we need to ask the right questions. Here's an exercise that will help you do just that. Ever since our boys were little, Valerie and I have strongly believed in the value of a weekend activity we call "The Sunday Search." We've been doing it for nearly twenty years now. We commend it as a kind of "game" for families or individuals. In the mid-1980s we began teaching it with David and Karen Mains as we ministered together on the daily radio broadcast *The Chapel of the Air.*

We like to think of The Sunday Search as a spiritual tool—a family resource, a doable weekly exercise—to help Moms and Dads and kids learn how to evaluate their Sunday experiences in a healthy way. If you learn to play The Sunday Search and do it regularly, it will enable you and your family—in fact, in a sense *force* you—to focus on the positive. That's because playing *The Sunday Search helps discipline you to ask the right questions in evaluating your weekly church experiences.*

THE SUNDAY SEARCH IN SCRIPTURE

In Hebrews 3:1 we're told, "Fix your thoughts on Jesus." He's the One worthy of honor. He's the One Who deserves our full attention—and this is especially true when we go to worship Him. And according to verse 6, "Christ is . . . over God's house. And we [who are believers] are His house."

Then in the remainder of Hebrews 3 we find that two specific expectations are placed on all Christians, stated in the form of warnings. First, in verse 8: "Do not harden your hearts . . . ." Rather, we are to *hear* the voice of the Lord. Said differently: Listen to what the Lord has to say to you!

The second expectation is found in verses 12 and 13: "See to it, brothers [and sisters], that none of you has a sinful, unbelieving heart that turns away from the living God. But encourage one another . . . ."

Two specific "life responses" are called for in this passage, and they serve as the basis for this resource tool—this family spiritual activity we call The Sunday Search. Stated in the form of questions, these guidelines, or expectations, outlined in Hebrews 3 direct us as we evaluate our church experience, to do so according to what's happening spiritually.

THE SUNDAY SEARCH IN THREE PARTS

- *Sunday Search Question #1:* Ask yourself, "In what way or ways did God speak to me?

Another way of asking this is: "What was said or sung or read in the service (or Sunday school class or children's church) that ministered to me so specifically, it was as if I heard God's voice?" The Spirit of God may use the words of a song or opening prayer to calm your anxieties. Or, during the time set aside for quiet, silent prayer, or sharing prayer concerns, the Lord may bring to your mind a forgotten commitment. The Lord might speak to you or your child throughout a Bible story, the reading of Scripture, a testimonial from another student, the pastor's sermon, during a musical presentation—communicated through a choir, a soloist, an ensemble. Your child may hear God's love through the kind words of another class member.

The possibilities are many. The point is, if you and your children are actively searching for a word from the Lord during a class or worship service, almost without fail He'll speak to you in one way or another.

- *Sunday Search Question #2:* Ask yourself, "In what way or ways did God speak *through* me?"

Or, incorporating the word used in Hebrews 3, another way of asking this is: "What did I say or do to *encourage* someone else—a seeker, a fellow believer or believers?"

It might be just a friendly glance or a gracious comment. The book of Proverbs reminds us that an appropriate word spoken at the right time "is like apples of gold in settings of silver."

God may also speak through you or your child when you offer your service to another. Your child may invite a visitor to come along. Your son may ask the new kid in his Sunday school class to sit with him. Your daughter could volunteer to show up early and help her leader set up the chairs or props needed for class. You could volunteer to help in the nursery. Providing someone a ride home, inviting a new family or single person over for lunch are other ways God could be speaking *through* you or your child.

Again, the two key words at the core of the big idea associated with The Sunday Search are *to* and *through.* They represent two of the right questions—*(1) How did God speak to you? (2) How might God have spoken through you?*—to be asked whenever evaluating your weekly church experience.

- Then finally, to round out The Sunday Search game, it's important to share your observations with someone else.

Literally *talk about* what happened—how God spoke *to* you, and how you think He may have spoken *through* you. In other words, consciously and intentionally discuss and evaluate what's transpired week by week.

Simply put: The Sunday Search is an ongoing family activity that generates natural, along-the-way spiritual conversation around three basic concepts or "rules" represented by *to, through,* and *talk about.*

MAKE IT YOUR OWN

An idea that's worked for our family over the long haul is to talk about our Sunday Search discoveries on the way home from church and/or around the dinner table. A discussion like this positively reinforces spiritual values and helps the whole family focus on *significant* rather that peripheral issues concerning what goes on at church.

We invite you and your family to start playing The Sunday Search game beginning this weekend. (And, of course, if you attend church services on Saturdays instead of Sundays, just call the game The Saturday Search! Doesn't matter. The concept works just the same.) Adopt it as your own. Instill it into your routine, the fabric of your family life. Make it a part of your weekend vocabulary when talking with family or friends.

I've barely scratched the surface in illustrating the ways God can speak *to* and *through* you and me. But think of the positive changes that might come about in your family's weekly church experience if, habitually, you were to leave the services reviewing in your mind how God spoke *to* you and how he might have spoken *through* you. At a bare minimum, if someone ever approached you at the end of a church service, asking, "Well, what did you think?" you and everyone in your family will at least know *the right questions* to answer!

Family Resource Article 3

"GETTING TO KNOW YOU": A FAMILY GAME

CREATING MEANINGFUL TABLE CONVERSATION

How many times have you experienced a social occasion with a group of people—perhaps work associates, friends or acquaintances of extended family members, a block party in the neighborhood, a church gathering, or a get-together of parents at a school function—only to have one person dominate the conversation throughout the entire dinner, reception, festivities, or evening? Likely there were a number of individuals you would have loved to get to know better, but it just didn't happen. Because Mr. or Ms. So-and-so couldn't stop talking! You were stuck.

Not exactly time well spent—at least that's how Valerie and I (and now both of our sons) react to such happenings. "Ugh! What was that about? That should have been fun, but it wasn't ... bummer!" we typically grouse back and forth once we're in the privacy of our car on the ride back home.

Over the years we've noticed a growing trend that appears to be on the rise—a lot of people (even church people!) aren't very accomplished at asking good questions. In fact some don't ever seem to initiate conversations at all. At least that's what our experience and anecdotal research indicates. It's as though the art of conversation has been lost—in society, in the church, and yes, even in our homes. How sad.

REVERSING THE TREND

The good news is: It doesn't have to be this way. And it's our conviction that from this point forward God's people can make an immediate positive difference in this arena in whatever settings you find yourself. How? By developing and honing your skills to become effective conversationalists, which can begin in your own home as you help your children learn how to ask meaningful questions.

Scripture is peppered with accounts of Jesus engaging in lively conversations with all kinds of people He met along the way—old, young, educated, uneducated, healthy, sick, men, women, rich, poor, religious, irreligious, and those of every nationality. He was approachable, responsive, interested, willing (or not) to take initiative as needed. The bottom line: Jesus was a winsome, dynamic, always appropriate, master communicator!

He asked great questions. Remember Jesus' encounter with the Samaritan woman at the well in John 4? Fascinating exchange. Also, He continually dialogued with His disciples, the religious leaders of the day, His supporters, His critics, the skeptics, as well as the pressing crowds who followed Him wherever He traveled. He is an "out-of-this-world model" for each of us!

A VARIETY OF BENEFITS

Let me introduce you to another family game that has been invaluable in the Bell household for more than twenty years now. It's a fun one! And the spin-off benefits we've discovered along the way have been multiple. This game

- accelerates a positive intensity in new relationships;
- develops a go-to bank of creative questions for you and family members to fall back on in new or maybe even awkward situations;
- creates a safe environment for some unexpected spiritual serendipities with people you hardly know;
- ensures that you don't talk too much yourself; and, best of all, . . .
- helps children learn how to participate in the art of significant conversation with peers and adults.

To date, this game that we've played hundreds of times has never been dubbed with an official name; here we'll simply call it the "Getting to Know You" game. Valerie's older sister, Karen Mains, and her family first introduced us to a version of this delightful activity back in the 1970s. Since then, we have played it whenever we have first-time guests in our home for a meal, and quite often we'll do this with new friends or first-time guests at a restaurant as well. It's a game you can play around the table while you eat. For us, every family member who's present participates—without exceptions!

THE RULES OF THE GAME

The typical set-up goes something like this:

"We have a family game that we always play whenever we invite guests to have a meal with us. It's quite simple. There are only two rules—and since you're our guests, we get to make up the rules!

"Here's Rule #1: While we're eating, we get to ask you any questions we want.

"And Rule #2: You have to answer our questions honestly—and we'll know whether or not you're telling us the truth!

"That's all there is to it. It couldn't be easier."

Then the fun begins.

To get the game going, we've always made it a practice in our family to let the youngest child present ask the first question; and the questioner also gets to choose to whom the question is directed. (Note: Only one of the guests answers each question.) Then the next Bell family member offers a different question to the person of his or her choice—that is, if more than one person is visiting with us; otherwise another question is directed to our solo guest.

We continue to work our way around the table, asking different questions of each visitor until all have participated. Then, time permitting, we start with another round of questions and continue on until the conversation has run its course. The number of guests at the table—and how long each person takes to respond—determines how many questions are actually asked.

Without fail, this table conversation exercise is always a hit! Plus, it's a fast and effective way to get to know people amazingly well in a relatively short amount of time.

All through their school years each of our boys would be upfront with their friends and forewarn them whenever they invited someone new to our house for a meal. "Don't be surprised—my folks and brother are going to ask you lots of questions over dinner. Don't worry. It's a family game we play that's actually sort of fun!" was the common word of warning they'd offer.

QUESTIONS TO GET STARTED

Enough explanation. What follows are some of our favorite questions that may be helpful if you choose to jump-start this family game around your dinner table at home—or the next time you go out to eat with a new group of folks. You are invited to use these questions promiscuously (i.e., randomly and at your whim)!

1. You have two weeks available to you, and money is no object. You can go anywhere in the world and take with you as many people as you'd like. Where do you go and whom do you take? (This is Justin's first question he has always asked from the time he was a five-year-old!)

2. Pretend you can shrink yourself down to an inch tall, and you could ride around in somebody's coat pocket for a day. In fact, if you'd like, you can go back in time and pick anybody who has ever lived. Whose pocket would you choose to ride around in and why? (And you don't have to say Jesus!)

3. This is a two-part question: In what ways are you most like your father? And in what ways are you most like your mother?

4. Talk about one of the happiest days of your life that, if you could, you'd like to live over again.

5. Another two-parter: If someone were going to write a book about your life up to this point, what would be an appropriate title? But then, if you could have extra time and make any changes in your life, tell us what you would wish the title to be.

6. Talk about both a movie and a book that have had a powerful impact or a disproportionate influence on your life.

7. If you have a completely free day at home to spend alone for replenishment—no obligations of any kind—how would you choose to use it?

8. For an unmarried guest: Tell us about the top five qualities you're looking for in a lifetime mate.

9. What was it about your spouse that first attracted you to him/her? Then tell us how you met each other.

10. If you were told you have to move—no longer can you live where you are now—where would you choose to go to settle down and why?

11. Describe one of your most embarrassing experiences—which you can tell all of us about!

12. If you could wave a magic wand that guaranteed three changes of your choice with immediate national impact would come to pass, what would you do?

13. You're given the opportunity to start all over again right out of high school, with the condition that you'd have to pursue a different career. What would be your new line of work you'd want to prepare for?

14. What biblical character do you most relate to and why?

15. Describe an incident from your childhood when you experienced an unusual sense of God's presence in your life.

16. What were the circumstances that brought you to the decision point of crossing the line of faith—to become a follower of Christ?

Well, you get the idea. There are literally hundreds of these kinds of questions to be asked that can lead to both meaningful and memorable—and ultimately spiritual—encounters for you, your family, and newfound friends. Not to mention the potential of discovering rich and significant relationships that may otherwise go untapped.

Do yourself a favor. Do your kids a favor. Do the church a favor. Hone the art of creating meaningful conversations—for the sake of the kingdom!

GOING THE DISTANCE WITH YOUR PRODIGAL CHILD

Marathon races have become increasingly popular in recent years. The runners—conditioned athletes who exert almost all their energy to finish the race—push themselves to the physical limits. And we on the sidelines applaud the tenacity and discipline of the human spirit.

Still, participating in a marathon is something most of us will likely never choose to do. Yet some parents among us may be called upon to run a different kind of marathon—one that demands more discipline and stamina than *any* athletic contest. Parents who must contend with wayward children—parents of prodigals—face an intense challenge indeed, anticipated by few and desired by no one.

In a very real sense the wayward child is an enigma. Trying to understand his or her struggles may take years, even a lifetime. At best this kind of family marathon is painful to all.

When I say *wayward,* I'm not talking about the child who occasionally disobeys or steps out of line. I don't mean the son who doesn't mow the grass when instructions are clearly given, or the daughter who comes home from her evening out with friends thirty minutes after curfew.

Instead, his or her behavior has become largely unpredictable. The wayward child or teenager generally makes decisions that contradict the desired or expected. This is the kid who appears to be deliberately following a certain course in life that may cause him or her to self-destruct—be it the abuse of drugs, alcohol, trouble with the law, promiscuity, homosexuality, whatever.

Parents of such offspring sometimes have their heartache compounded by hearing other adults (even Christians, occasionally) suggest that wayward children are always the product of irresponsible parents. Let me assure, however, those are snap judgments and overly simplistic assumptions. Remember, even Adam and Eve's firstborn was wayward—Cain murdered his very own brother. Imagine how devastated Adam and Eve must have felt. Their pain had to be unbearably overwhelming.

Perhaps you find yourself running in this kind of marathon. As far as you can tell it's a race without a finish line. You're not sure where to turn, and the situation appears hopeless. Yet you *long* to be a loving parent. But how?

AN EXAMPLE FROM SCRIPTURE

Jesus has suggested the answer in His famous story of the prodigal son. Though it's a familiar account, let me highlight a few observations.

The story begins with the problem: the younger of two sons demanded from his father his share of the estate early. That was a gutsy request to say the least, and this was a home of considerable wealth. Now, Jesus didn't say it, but it should be obvious that this boy wasn't looking out for his family. Nor was he terribly concerned about the feelings or reputation of his parents. And for his father to lay out that much capital all at once could conceivably jeopardize the family business . . . and on top of that, what would people say?! To put it plainly, this was a self-centered, I'm-gonna-do-my-thing-my-way kid.

So how did his father respond? "No way . . . over my dead body young man!" No, that's not what he said. "What? Don't you have any common sense for what's proper? You're grounded for two months!" He didn't respond this way either.

Instead, he gave in to his son's request, reluctantly perhaps, and probably not until he explained all the possible consequences. But Jesus tells us the father divided his property between them. Despite the inconvenience and embarrassment of the situation, the father continued loving his son! Apparently this man had recognized his child was an independent individual with the capacity to make his own decisions. Evidently he realized that no matter how hard he tried, he could not force his child to buy in to his value system. So he let him go.

The son left home with the jingle in his pocket, and he did his thing. He had the time of his life. You know the story—travel, friends, the nightlife, wild parties, booze, prostitutes—he did it all. In the meantime, what about Dad? Though he had completely lost the whereabouts of his son, don't think for a minute he had dismissed his son from his mind. The empty chair at the dinner table, the vacant bedroom, the absent partner in the family business, plus the significant strain on the reserves and family's cash flow—all served as daily reminders that his child had gone astray.

It's interesting that we're never told how much time was involved before the prodigal son came to the end of himself and began his turnaround. It could have been years—two, three, five, who knows? Jesus didn't say. Also, no specifics are mentioned concerning the intensity of the turmoil experienced by the father, but who of us would doubt that it was there? Oh, life went on, but not without pain. I'm sure he felt it deeply. So how did he deal with it? He hoped . . . he waited . . . and waited . . . patiently. His hope was persistent, tenacious.

Well, the son finally came to his senses. But not until he hit bottom. Living among pigs, hungry, depressed, forsaken, and miserable, he remembered the sweetness of home. So, humbly, he began his journey back. Jesus described this return: "But while he was still a long way off, his father saw him and was filled with compassion for him" (Luke 15:20a).

Now this was a dad who had gone the distance. His love was unconditional. He had accepted his own personal discomfort and was prepared to offer forgiveness and welcome back his child. Jesus said,

"He ran to his son, threw his arms around him and kissed him" (v. 20b). The child, at his own initiative, chose to repent and a great celebration followed.

CHOOSING TO GO THE DISTANCE

The ever-constant, nonnegotiable parenting lesson in all of this—that jumps off the pages of Scripture—is: *Loving parents choose to go the distance with each child regardless of his or her life's choices.* Sooner or later our children will make their own decisions. As parents our role all along is to love them, support them, accept them as they are (yes, with all their idiosyncrasies!) and, as best we can, show them the way to go.

We cannot always control our children. But we can determine to go the distance with our children regardless of their choices.

Clearly, the situation will be difficult. You may have to swallow huge lumps of pride. In fact, you may be misunderstood by people within your closest circles, from your own church, even by some well-intended friends. How should you respond—to your child and to others?

Remember, your focus is always on your child, not the responses of others. You know, and God knows, the truth. So what can you do to help? Show kindness to your child. Accept him or her, while disapproving of the choices. For you, that might mean reaching out in kindness to your grown child's live-in companion. It doesn't mean you have to approve of the relationship, but discarding your child in the process is *not* an alternative.

Accept the facts for what they are. Going the distance in your case might require attending endless group sessions for alcoholics in an attempt to support your son or daughter; or spending hundreds, even thousands of dollars, for professional counseling. That's right, you and your child side-by-side being vulnerable with someone who can help you resolve those long-standing issues or conflicts. For someone else, going the distance will involve raising a grandchild born out of wedlock; or trying to pick up the pieces of a broken marriage that you disapproved of from the very beginning.

What I'm suggesting is not a "well, kid, you're just going to have to buck up and suffer the consequences" type of attitude; you can be certain your child will experience a fair share of pain without your piling on more. Rather, if ever called upon for such a marathon, may God give you the grace and courage and stamina to say: "Whatever it takes, regardless of the personal inconvenience or complexities of the situation, you can count on me. I'll be there, available to do everything I can."

I want to encourage you who are in the heat of the race. Though none of us can predict the eventual outcome, and while there are no guarantees to be offered—maybe, just maybe, someday that wayward son or daughter will come back, repentant and changed. So please—as tired as you may be, and even if you feel like giving up—don't bolt the door of your home or your heart. I have a feeling you may discover there *really is hope*. Grab hold of it and don't let go!

MORE THAN A PARABLE

We conclude with an unedited, tell-all, straightforward letter from two parents we know personally. Doug and Madeline (not their real names) have actually experienced what it means to go the distance with a prodigal child. Read it and discover anew that when God is involved, there really is hope.

Dear Discouraged Parent,

Are you frustrated, bewildered, angry, hurt, guilt-ridden, humiliated and feeling that you are a total failure as a parent? Please sit down and pour yourself a cup of coffee while we unmask our feelings and relate how pain partially paralyzed us.

As a young Christian couple, we looked forward to the day we would be parents. We knew that this would be a big responsibility, but never dreamed it would be so overwhelming. It was an exhausting roller-coaster ride for nearly sixteen years.

We found God to be our stabilizer when the earth was crumbling beneath us. Perhaps crisis in our family helped us anchor to that One who is solid, the Lord Jesus Christ. He cares and knows what it is to hurt. We write this letter greatly hoping to encourage you as you confront a similar situation at your home.

In relating to the wayward child, we first want to share early observations and warnings, and then list some dos and don'ts that we experienced which may be of benefit to you.

Our child was super-active from an early age. He was not destructive, but his mind was always thinking way ahead of ours. We tried to curb this aggressiveness through discipline, but we should have spent more time in challenging and channeling his aggressive motives into positive gestures rather than trying to "tame" them. This would have helped to build a more positive self-image for him.

The hours he spent in school were disastrous. We were intimidated by his teachers and principals. The character building was negative. They did not seek any positive actions or results in our son. They expected all discipline to be implemented at home. Consequently, the child not only failed at school, but also faced discipline for that failure at home. It doesn't take long for a child to label himself as "different," an "outcast," and a "failure."

Today we would demand more time, consult with the teachers and principals, and work together to construct a more positive self-image for our son. We would select his teachers each year in the elementary grades. Some teachers are better trained to help the active child. This action possibly would have spared him the necessity of entering a special education program and the need for prescribed drugs. We realize this now, because today he handles learning and job training very well without any special attention or drugs.

Another problem we faced was his drug addiction. When do you suspect a child may be taking drugs? Professionals can give you advice on this subject, but allow us to acquaint you with a few of the symptoms we noticed. Eating habits change; usually no appetite. Attitudes and personalities are anything but pleasant. Behavior patterns worsen.

What can we do when our child is on drugs? As with any rebellious behavior, we need to make certain we tell him of the choice he is making; the harm it will do physically and mentally; the terrible addiction it can produce; and its danger for not only his life but possibly to others as well. He is making a choice that could affect his life forever. We should audibly pray with the child, asking God to take away the sinful desire. He must realize that we are praying daily for him to make the right choice.

When our child has chosen to continue the drug or alcohol route, what is next? We begin to cry out for help. Prior to finding prayer support partners, we seek every possible solution. "Oh, if I could get him into this Christian school or into that professional clinic; that will take care of the problem." Time passes. Hundreds, even thousands, of dollars are spent—and the problem is still there.

What happens at this point? No success! Feelings of exhaustion, guilt, pain, frustration and failure set in. Other members of the family feel neglected, and we are tempted to blame each other for the problems. We avoid socializing with friends because we have too much pride to share our hurts. Going to church is depressing; school, medical experts, and police authorities have failed; and each day is consumed by these problems. Have you ever felt any of these hurts?

We really hesitate to even use this phrase because it has become such a worn-out cliché—but it finally became real to us: "Let go . . . let God." Once we let go of the situation, we began to open up to friends. We began to have prayer support from all over the country. We could feel the very presence of God. We totally committed our son to God. We stepped back and began to watch. No, the problem did not cease, but we were able to free ourselves of guilt, shame, frustration and failure—to lift our heads once again.

The prodigal son in the Bible chose to leave home. Our prodigal son was asked to leave. After exhausting all possible solutions, with the help of our pastor, we drew a line which if crossed, he would be asked to leave home. We hope that your situation will not dictate this kind of action. For us, this was the last solution and the most painful. However, we did this with love and with no regrets. This is not the answer for everyone.

We began praying that Satan would be bound; that he would not be allowed to harm our son. God answered our prayers. Our son's life was spared many times, and we are sure that the guardian angels were working overtime. We felt strongly that God would bring our son unto Himself. We didn't know how or when or by whom, but we had that assurance for those sixteen years. We never gave up hope. [Through the influence of believers in another part of the country, our son eventually came to faith in Christ, and our relationship with him has been fully restored.]

Let us give you a few suggestions, which may help you through these trying days:

1. Share with someone.
2. Let God have full control.
3. Love unconditionally.
4. Don't allow Satan to break up the family.
5. Pray that Satan will be bound, so that no harm will come to the child.
6. Pray expectantly.
7. Let the following verses help you as they helped us:

What a wonderful God we have—he is the Father of our Lord Jesus Christ, the source of every mercy, and the one who so wonderfully comforts and strengthens us in our hardships and trials. And why does he do this? So that when others are troubled, needing our sympathy and encouragement, we can pass on to them this same help and comfort God has given us. You can be sure that the more we undergo sufferings for Christ, the more he will shower us with his comfort and encouragement. We are in deep trouble for bringing you God's comfort and salvation. But in our trouble God had comforted us—and this, too, to help you: to show you from our personal experience how God will tenderly comfort you when you undergo these same sufferings. *He will give you the strength to endure"* (2 Corinthians 1:3–7 TLB, emphasis added).

It's our prayer that we have been some help to you. Though it's not the path we ever would have chosen, God has been so gracious to us and we feel privileged to have this opportunity to share our testimony with you.

> With God's ever-present love,
> Doug and Madeline

Moody Press, a ministry of Moody Bible Institute,
is designed for education, evangelization, and edification.
If we may assist you in knowing more about Christ
and the Christian life, please write us without obligation:
Moody Press, c/o MLM, Chicago, Illinois 60610.

More Quality Books from Moody Press and Steve & Valerie Bell

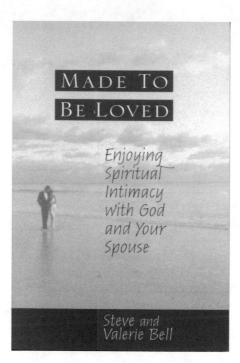

Made to Be Loved
Enjoying Spiritual Intimacy with God and Your Spouse

Do you want more - more meaning, more caring, more understanding in your marriage? The answer is simple yet many Christians end up trapped in hollow, hurtful marriages. Steve and Valerie Bell were well on their way to having such a dissatisfactory union when they learned the key to a fantastic marriage: spiritual intimacy. Sharing the tools that worked for them, the Bells have worked out seven spiritual intimacy exercises to help you form a greater attachment to God and your mate.

ISBN #0-8024-3399-5, Paperback

Learn More about Raising Spiritually Healthy Children

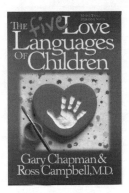

The Five Love Languages of Children
By Gary Chapman & Ross Campbell, MD
More than 300,000 in print

Each child, like an adult, expresses and receives love best through one of five different communication styles. This truth can work against parents who speak different love languages than their children. However, when properly prepared, moms and dads can use this information to help them meet their children's deepest emotional needs.
ISBN #1-881273-65-2, Paperback

A Gift from God
Foundational Principles of Biblical Parenting
By Dr. Larry Mercer

God places in parent's hands a special person He intentionally created, gave unique gifts, and authorized a special mission for their life as a gift to us. Dr. Mercer guides parents in putting aside their own agendas for our children, and teaches them how to embrace the challenges and joys of helping our children fulfill God's plan for their lives.

ISBN #0-8024-1441-9, Paperback

Light Their Fire for God
7 Powerful Virtues for your Kids
By Anne and David Harper

Parenting is an awesome responsibility. As a mom or dad, it's your job to make sure your child's physical, emotional, and even social needs are met. But, like many parents, you may find that the most daunting task of all is that of shepherding your son or daughter's spiritual life. Filled with practical parenting tips for everyday family life, as well as valuable scriptural insights, *Light Their Fire for God* will develop your child's life.
ISBN #0-8024-4292-7, Paperback

ADDITIONAL RESOURCES FROM THE BELLS

If you are interested in contacting Steve and/or Valerie Bell about speaking at your church, organization, or special event, write or call at:

Steve or Valerie
P.O. Box 1399
Wheaton, Illinois 60189
Fax/Phone: 630/688-8412

To learn how you can obtain other books by the Bells, as well as audio and videotape resources represented by those listed below, please write or call. Other available materials include:

Made to Be Loved: Enjoying Spiritual Intimacy with God and Your Spouse (book)
A Well-Tended Soul: Staying Beautiful for the Rest of Your Life (book)
She Can Laugh at the Days to Come: Strengthening the Soul for the Journey Ahead (book)
Getting Out of Your Kids' Faces and into Their Hearts: Become the Warm, Loving Parent You've Always Wanted to Be (book)
Getting Out of Your Kids' Faces and into Their Hearts (four-part video series)
Reaching Out to Lonely Kids: A Guide to Surviving and Loving the Children in Your Neighborhood (book)
Coming Back: Real-life Stories of Courage from Spiritual Survivors (book)
Back to Your Spiritual Future: Recapturing "First Love" Intensity in Your Relationship with Christ (book)
Two Are Better Than One: A Guide to Prayer Partnerships That Work (book)
PRAYERWALK . . . Care for Body and Soul (aerobic audio/music cassette)
PRAYERWALK II . . . Praise, the Practice of Heaven (aerobic audio/music cassette)
CLASSIC PRAYERWALK . . . Blessing Your Community (aerobic audio/music cassette)

THIS RESOURCE WAS CREATED TO SERVE YOU . . .

It is just one of many ministry tools that are part of the Willow Creek Resources® line, published by the Willow Creek Association together with Moody Press. The Willow Creek Association (WCA) was created in 1992 to serve a rapidly growing number of churches from all across the denominational spectrum that are committed to helping unchurched people become fully devoted followers of Christ. Membership in the WCA now numbers over 6,400 churches worldwide.

The Willow Creek Association links like-minded Christian leaders with each other and with strategic vision, training, and resources in order to help them build prevailing churches. Here are some of the ways it does that:

Prevailing Church Conferences—a biannual two-and-a-half days event, held at Willow Creek Community Church in South Barrington, Ill., that are being used by God to help pioneering church leaders find new and innovative ways to build prevailing churches that reach unchurched people.

The Leadership Summit—a once-a-year event designed to increase the leadership effectiveness of pastors, ministry staff, volunteer church leaders, and Christians in business.

Willow Creek Resources®—to provide churches with a trusted channel of ministry resources in areas of leadership, evangelism, spiritual formation, spiritual gifts, small groups, the use of the arts—drama, contemporary music, and more. For more information about Willow Creek Resources® call Willow Direct at 800/570-9812. Outside the U.S. call 847/765-0070.

WCA News—a bimonthly newsletter to inform you of the latest trends, resources, and information on WCA events from around the world.

The Exchange—our online classified ads service to assist churches in recruiting key staff for ministry positions.

WillowNet—an Internet resource service that provides access to hundreds of transcripts of Willow Creek messages, drama sketches, songs, videos and multimedia suggestions. The system allows users to sort through these elements and download them for a fee.

Defining Moments—a monthly hour-long audio journal for church leaders featuring Bill Hybels and other Christian leaders discussing probing issues to help you discover biblical principles and transferable strategies to maximize your church's redemptive potential.

For specific information about WCA membership, upcoming conferences and other ministry services contact:

Willow Creek Association
P.O. Box 3188
Barrington, IL 60011-3188
Phone: 847/765-0070
Fax: 847/765-5046
www.willowcreek.com